Extravagant Breakthroughs

Sue Sinclair

First Published in United Kingdom, 2020

British Library Cataloguing-in-Publication Data. A catalogue record for this book is available from the British Library

ISBN: 978-1-908154-48-4

Cover Design: Esther Kotecha, EKDesigns
Typeset by Angela Selfe
Printed in the United Kingdom

Table of Contents

THANK YOU TO . . .

My precious and amazing husband Steve who enables, encourages, releases and cheers me on to do all that I do. You are my super hero!

All of the incredible Community Watchmen Ministries (CWM) Team – you are true heroes and I love that we get to experience these adventures together both home and away! Huge thanks to all who have encouraged and helped with the editing, your skills and vision for *Extravagant Breakthroughs* has continued to inspire me. Special thanks to Pam Shaw, Rosemary Burden, Jan Cornish, Tracey Spiers, Ian and Ali Rimmer and of course David Powell who has published this for me.

All those in Uganda, South Africa, Rwanda and Ghana who enabled us to serve alongside you in your beautiful nations. Massive thanks to my incredible and courageous travelling companions who were willing to go on the adventures!

Thank you to our precious friends Archbishop Justice and Maria, who love Cape Coast so much they dared to challenge mindsets to bring about repentance and the start of healing.

I want to acknowledge and honour the amazing Papa Alfie Fabe, who impacted our lives so much both here in Liverpool and out in Cape Town, South Africa. Papa Fabe went to be with Jesus on 30th July 2020 and left behind a huge legacy.

I especially want to thank God and to give Him all the glory for every breakthrough and for the fruit to come.

ENDORSEMENTS

Sue Sinclair's *Extravagant Breakthroughs* is a testimony of God's amazing interventions with many different groups and situations. Sue recalls the many breakthroughs in Liverpool and Africa that she has been part of. In Isaiah 6:8 (ASV) it says: *"And I heard the voice of the Lord saying, 'Whom shall I send, and who will go for us?' Then I said, 'Here am I! Send me'"*. Sue certainly has answered that call and her obedience and willingness to say "Yes" has opened many doors and places she could never have dreamed of going to. The fact is, Sue carries God's breakthroughs because she carries God's Spirit. As a prophet and intercessor, she has insight into the different situations she finds herself in. This book will encourage you; it will provoke you for more and it will have you marvelling at God's interventions.

Tim Eldridge
Co-Founder & Director of Presence Ministries International
www.presenceministriesinternational.org

I have known Sue for over 25 years. Our paths have often crossed as she has been so instrumental in leading the inter-church prayer initiative in Liverpool, and I led the prayer movement in Manchester for a period of ten years.

Extravagant Breakthroughs is a book born out of real experience, both in her home City of Liverpool and her travels around the globe. Of particular interest today is her chapter which talks about praying about the transatlantic slave trade and its impact upon Liverpool.

Sue has experienced times of breakthrough and you can too.

Debra Green OBE
Director, Redeeming Our Communities

Sue's journey from brokenness and insecurity as a child to become a mature prophetic voice in our city, nation, and across the world is nothing short of extraordinary. I felt exhausted and thrilled at the same time to read of so many accounts of God's amazing timings, divine appointments, and supernaturally opened doors. This book is full of stories of extravagant breakthroughs.

From her home city of Liverpool, where this journey began, Sue has been criss-crossing the continent of Africa, and ministering in the USA. God has used Sue and her team to speak not only to police chiefs, justices, bishops, and government leaders, but also to minister healing and love to some of the most seemingly insignificant and downtrodden members of society.

The ongoing story of liberation from the generational influences of the transatlantic slave trade is a central theme to this book, and God has woven the thread of Sue's life into the fabric of his healing of the nations from this blight on Africa, Europe and the USA.

It is no coincidence that God has chosen someone raised in Liverpool, a city at the heart of the slave trade, to pull down so many of the strongholds of slavery across the nations affected by it. I am grateful to Sue's obedience to her prophetic and intercessory calling and am glad for this book that brings another chapter to this unfolding story of healing, liberation, and transformation.

Dr Nic Harding
Director of Together for the Harvest, a 'unity for mission' movement in the Liverpool City Region

Sue is the real deal. She has an Ephesians 4 gift of a Prophet, not just an ability to prophecy, which she has used for many years here in the Liverpool City Region and also as the Spirit has led, in other Nations. Her desire is to speak the word of God, seeking God for breakthrough in the heavens and spiritual realms, as well as here on earth. She has experienced God's favour, through her willingness to intercede and pray, gathering others around her, crying out on behalf of cites and nations. God has heard her cry and is healing the land and the city. This book highlights her obedience to God and her willingness to be used in 'Extravagant Breakthroughs'. It is a great read about ordinary people being used by an extraordinary God to bring about change and breakthrough. This book will help us all fulfil the call upon God's church to "rebuild the ancient ruins and restore the places long devastated; they will renew the ruined cities that have been devastated for generations". Happy reading.

The Venerable Mike McGurk
Archdeacon of Liverpool

FOREWORD

It is an honour and joy to be invited to write a Foreword to this inspiring book, *Extravagant Breakthroughs*. It is additionally heart-warming because of my involvement in some of the narratives, when I had previously shied away from this kind of exercise.

During the celebration in the UK of the 200th Anniversary of the Abolition of the Slave Trade in 2007, I was one of the three Anglican Archbishops – Canterbury, West Africa and West Indies — representing the three hotspots of the transatlantic slave trade. The expected follow-up programme in my province was a failure, as both religious and secular leaders showed no interest. I had to retire a few years later and thought that was the end of my involvement in the issue of the slave trade in Africa.

My wife Maria had to move in the mid-90s to Liverpool to continue her medical education and was shocked to see Liverpool as dilapidated as Cape Coast, her hometown. With the passage of time, Maria saw the transformation of Liverpool and wondered why and how? Her search led to Sue Sinclair and Community Watchmen Ministries. This is when we got to know of the journey of prayer and repentance the people of Liverpool had been on for years. We discovered the stark truth that every place involved in the slave trade historically, had been broken and it was only repentance and reconciliation that would bring cleansing and healing.

The book *Extravagant Breakthroughs* contains the road map that God has used to deal with the wounds of the slave trade, including orphan and poverty spirits, powerlessness and disunity not only in Liverpool but Uganda, South Africa, Rwanda and Ghana.

Even though I was involved in the three years of preparatory work, it was emotionally moving to read Sue's description of the service of Public Apology and Repentance. This involved the church, the traditional leaders (chiefs) and the government; such co-operation or unity having been an anathema to these people in the past, because we did not want to accept the part we played in selling our brothers and sisters.

Aptly, Sue shares how she had to overcome the fears and anxieties associated with her call, and her tried and tested experiences that shaped her, and could shape anyone desirous of being a vessel of transformation of individuals and communities. In the process, Sue expresses her dependency on the intercession of the members of CWM and her unalloyed thanks to them.

This appreciation and dependency reminds me of the words of Max Lucado:

> "Our prayers may be awkward.
> Our attempts may be feeble.
> But since the power of prayer is in the one who hears it and not in the one who says it
> Our prayers do make a difference."[1]

---

1. Max Lucado, *He Still Moves Stones* (Nashville TN: Thomas Nelson, 2013)

In the end, be encouraged in your spiritual journey by the writer's mantra "it is good to be in the right place, at the right time, with the right people, doing the right thing".

Most Rev'd Justice O. Akrofi
Emeritus Archbishop
Province of West Africa

The Greatest Breakthrough Ever

The Oxford Dictionary describes "Breakthrough" as a sudden, dramatic and important discovery or development.

The Bible is full of stories of breakthroughs. However, the greatest breakthrough that ever was and ever will be, was Jesus' birth, death and dramatic resurrection from the dead. God's plan was always that we were created to rule and reign with Him. However, Satan's plan was always to confuse God's people so that they unwittingly handed over their authority to him. You can read this story in Genesis 2:15 to Genesis 3:24. Man and woman continued to mess up and, despite God giving Moses a set of commandments to help everyone to live righteously, they still made wrong choices.

Thankfully God had a master plan to bring into action, because He knew we would never be good enough to come into His holy presence. For many hundreds of years, each time the Children of Israel sinned they would take a pure spotless lamb and that would be sacrificed to God on their behalf, to pay for every sin they committed. However, they continued to sin, and God knew He needed a better sacrifice.

The Bible tells us that, at the right time, Jesus the Son of God left heaven and came to earth as a tiny vulnerable baby. Wow! Now that was a massive breakthrough because He was conceived in Mary's womb without any help from any earthly man. He was a miracle baby for sure!

Jesus was baptised when he was thirty, by his cousin known as John the Baptist. This is recorded in John 1:29 *"John saw Jesus coming towards him to be baptised and said, 'Look, the Lamb of God, who takes away the sin of the world!'"*

Immediately after that, Jesus, filled with the Holy Spirit, was able to resist Satan when He was tempted in the desert. Jesus came out of that time of temptation still filled with the Holy Spirit. He was then ready to begin his earthly ministry of releasing heaven to earth. Challenging the norm of the day in every way, He brought breakthrough every day – healing the sick, raising the dead, setting those with demons free, transforming lives and performing miracles. He was, still is, and will always be the Master of extravagant breakthrough.

John was one of Jesus' disciples and he recorded that Jesus himself declared, *"I tell you this timeless truth: The person who follows me in faith, believing in me, will do the same mighty miracles that I do—even greater miracles than these because I go to be with my Father!"* John 14:12 (TPT). The question and challenge for us is . . . how many of us do?

The disciples would not have understood what Jesus meant when he said, *"Because I go to be with my Father"*. However, we have the incredible gift of hindsight because this was recorded for us in the Gospels and other books of the Bible. We can read about Jesus' death on the cross, and how He was raised to life again before He ascended back to heaven to be with our Heavenly Father. It is all written there to read and yet we often fail to understand what that means for us, for the Church and for the world we live in. We read it as a story and not as a reality!

Jesus died upon a cross like many other people in the Roman times. However, that is where the comparison ends! Everyone else died because of their sin or because they had upset the Romans, but Jesus' death was very different. The Bible tells us that when Jesus' body was nailed up on to the huge wooden cross and lifted into position, at 9am in the morning, God poured upon him the sin of the whole world. Jesus, the pure spotless lamb, was loaded down with my sin and your sin. He was loaded down with every sin ever committed, from creation to the day that Jesus the Bridegroom returns for His Bride. With the weight of the world's sin upon him as he hung upon the cross, Jesus died an excruciating death.

A number of years ago, God gave me a dance with some simple movements to a song by Leanne Rimes called "Ten thousand angels cried". I listened to it so many times and wept and wept and wept every time, as God gave me some revelation of what happened to Jesus.

> Stillness filled the heavens, on crucifixion day.
> Some say it rained, I don't know if it's true.
> Well, I can just imagine ten thousand angels cried
> That would seem like rain to me and you.
>
> The angels all stood ready to take him from the tree
> They waited for the words from his voice.
> And when he asked the father "Why has thou forsaken me?"
> They watched the Saviour die of his own choice.
>
> I've never seen ten thousand angels cry
> But I'm sure they did as they stood by
> And watched the Saviour die.
> God turned his head away
> He couldn't bear the sight
> It must have looked like rain
> When ten thousand angels cried.

As the sun slipped away
The skies turned to grey
And when Jesus gave his all
That's when the tears began to fall[2]

Jesus chose to die on the cross, releasing forgiveness to those around Him including you and me: that was the most powerful moment this world has ever known! At twelve noon the whole world turned dark, no lights or stars shining. Can you imagine the whole world suddenly turning dark in the middle of the day for at least three hours! Nothing like that had ever happened before and people would have been terrified.

In the midst of that darkness, at 3pm our precious Saviour Jesus breathed out his last breath. The power of God touched earth as Jesus's spirit, turned to the mocking Satan who thought he had accomplished the greatest defeat ever. In that incredible moment of extravagant breakthrough, Jesus took back the power and authority that Adam and Eve had handed over to Satan in the Garden of Eden. The breakthrough was so powerful that it caused the tectonic plates of the world to shift and there was a huge earthquake. Such was the power of God released upon the earth in that moment of breakthrough, that lots of graves opened and many holy people were raised back to life again. One of the greatest breakthroughs that happened at that time was when the power of God hit the Temple.

God was considered so holy, that only the High Priest was ever allowed to go behind the huge curtain, into the inner sanctuary of the Temple. The curtain itself was four inches thick, sixty feet in height and thirty feet wide, created in purple, scarlet and blue fabric. It was so big and heavy it took three hundred priests to move it. The Priest would go in on behalf of all of the people, wearing a beautiful garment that had bells, blue and purple pomegranates, and scarlet material attached to the bottom. As long as those outside could hear the tinkling of the bells, they would know the

---

2. Leanne Rimes, "Ten Thousand Angels Cried" from album *You Light Up My Life: Inspirational Songs* (Curb Records, 1997)

Priest was still alive. However, our heavenly Father did not create us to be apart from Him, divided by a curtain. So, as Jesus died and God's power touched the earth, God's presence tore the huge and very thick temple curtain from top to bottom. The curtain that separated man from God's presence was torn from the top to the bottom!! God moved out, never again to dwell in a temple made with earthly hands.

Jesus' precious broken body was taken down from the cross and stored in a cave with a huge stone rolled over the entrance to prevent anyone from stealing his body. Three days later there was another miraculous extravagant breakthrough: Jesus was raised from the dead and he walked, talked and met many people.

Jesus paid the price and opened the way for every one of us to encounter God's presence. Now we can be empowered to live in relationship every day with God our heavenly Father. If that was not enough, we can also be filled, fired and fuelled by the same Spirit that raised Jesus from the dead, the Holy Spirit.

Wow that is extravagant breakthrough! We now have a choice. We can either live a life of mediocracy, like those who trusted in the Priest who went into the Temple on their behalf, or we can choose to receive the gift of salvation by giving our whole life to Jesus and receiving our very own extravagant breakthrough from our heavenly Father. If you would like to do that here is a prayer you can pray:

> *Dear God, I know that I am a sinner and I am sorry for all the things I have done wrong. Thank you that when you died on the cross you paid the price for my sin. Today I give you my life and I am grateful that you have promised to receive me despite my many sins and failures. Heavenly Father, I take you at your word. I thank you that I can face death now that you are my Saviour. I ask you to fill me with your Holy Spirit, to empower me for living my life with you. Thank you for hearing my prayer. In Jesus' Name. Amen.*

The scene is now set for you to live a life of extravagant breakthroughs. You can also be a vessel that not only brings extravagant breakthroughs as you release heaven to earth, but you can bring great glory to God. God is looking for those who will choose to listen to Him and to do all that He calls them to do. However, so often there is no one strategy for breakthrough, it is all about listening to God and allowing Him to guide you. He is looking for those that He can fill with His love and who will be willing to share that love so that many people can know Him. Our heavenly Father is looking for those He can empower to do greater things than Jesus ever did. Are you willing and available?

The Bible is full of incredible stories of sudden, dramatic and important discoveries and developments. The good news is that God is still positioning His people for personal extravagant breakthroughs and to bring breakthroughs to others. I want to share some incredible modern stories of the breakthroughs we have been experiencing and the things that the Lord has been teaching us in the process. Get yourself ready! You may find yourself experiencing breakthroughs as you read this and put the simple principles I share into action.

Personally, I found that God wanted to bring so many breakthroughs in my life before He could really use me to bring breakthrough anywhere else. We have to be willing to allow the Lord to search our hearts and to empower us to deal with anything hindering us. A simple example for me was that I could not be used by God to go to the nation or the nations when I was crippled with a fear of travelling!

I do not know where the fear came from as I had not been in a car accident, but I do know it was causing me a lot of problems. I remember when my children were young, making them stand with me in the rain, getting soaked as we waited for the bus to go to school. Plenty of people have to do that, and you may be thinking, what is wrong with that? But you see, my car was sitting outside of the house and I was refusing to drive it. I was too scared to get behind the wheel and switch it on! If that was not bad enough, my Dad was very poorly in hospital and I needed to take two buses to get there almost every day. This situation was desperate, as I never knew when I would need to get to the hospital quickly. I knew I needed a real breakthrough!

When you need a breakthrough, there is only one place to go and that is to Jesus. I began my conversation, "Jesus if you would stop all the large wagons that drive on the dual carriageway on the way to my children's school, just until I get my confidence back, I will get in my car and drive". The moment I got behind the steering wheel of my car I was still terrified and gripped the steering wheel so tightly, my knuckles were white! I could hardly breathe, and my legs were shaking, but I had made a deal with Jesus and despite still being afraid, I was going to trust Him to set me free.

I switched the car engine on and did all the vehicle checks before pulling slowly away from the kerb. At the end of the road I needed to turn right! Help, that meant I had to cross the traffic to the opposite side of the road. Turning left would have been so much easier. My heart was beating so loud I thought it was going to jump out of my chest! The next big challenge was the very busy roundabout where the wagons would be thundering by. "Help me Jesus, please help me!" I quickly cried out. Then it happened, the first miracle – the roads leading into the roundabout were empty. The second miracle happened as I came off at the fourth exit on to the dual carriageway, normally filled with thundering wagons – that too was empty! No wagons or cars, completely empty. I quickly whispered, "Thank you Jesus".

From that day I would get into the car and put my trust in Jesus, as I prayed and prayed for wisdom and protection. Each day as I got to the roundabout there were no cars or wagons and the dual carriageway was empty. Little by little, I began to gain my confidence and the grip of fear began to diminish. Then gradually, God began to allow some traffic back on to my roundabout and my dual carriageway.

You see, we need to look fear in the eye, disempower it and declare it has no hold over us, even if it is only one day at a time. My breakthrough came because I would not allow myself to be crippled by fear any longer. What I did not know at the time, was that God had many travel plans in mind for me and He needed me to choose to be brave and courageous in order to shake off the fear.

> *"Have I not commanded you? Be strong and courageous. Do not be afraid; do not be discouraged, for the Lord your God will be with you wherever you go."* Joshua 1:9

Paul wrote to the people of Galatia (now Turkey) and it was recorded for us in Galatians 5:1:

> *"It is for freedom that Christ has set us free. Stand firm, then, and do not let yourselves be burdened again by a yoke of slavery".*

With God's help I was set free from the fear of driving and travelling, but I have to choose every day to stay free! Are there some things that you need to allow God to help you with? You see, when we remain fearful, we are actually choosing to be enslaved to the things that cause us to be frightened. Today, choose freedom and take hold of your breakthrough!

KEYS TO BREAKTHROUGH

I would love to say "just do this" and your breakthrough will come, but it is not like that. As you will read in the stories I share, every situation is unique and each breakthrough comes in a different way. However, I can share some principles that may help you:

- Walk close to Jesus and listen to Him.
- Do not make assumptions or move in presumption.
- Be patient and persevere.

- Be courageous when you know Jesus has called you.
- Face your fears and push through them.
- Do what Jesus tells you, no more and no less.
- Do what Jesus tells you, even when you do not understand.
- Take the first step, even when you cannot see the whole plan.
- Do what Jesus tells you, when He tells you.
- God's timing is not our timing, so stay alert.
- Keep watching for the breakthrough.
- Keep a record, notes, video and photographs where possible.
- Always give God the glory!

PRAYER: Heavenly Father I give you any fears that have been controlling my life. I ask you to give me courage to take those first steps to freedom and I trust that you will be with me every step of the way. Amen.

Focussed For Breakthrough

Many people have asked me in the midst of life's ups and downs, how do you stay focussed? That is such a great question because it is easy on the good days to keep running the race, even if you feel it is more of a plod than a sprint! Personally, I have found that on the very tough days, when I just want to withdraw and pull the duvet cover over my head, it is the vision that God has given me that keeps me going. For me, God speaks very clearly through dreams, visions and massive life-changing encounters.

When Steve and I first went to church, I became increasingly frustrated, because I had signed up for "Acts 2 Christianity". I believed Christians should be demonstrating the Biblical signs, wonders and miracles that Jesus said we would all be able to do. I certainly did not become a Christian to fill a pew or to just get my ticket to heaven. I signed up for a relationship with the living God, for salvation and so much more. It is sad to say that at that time I did not see many signs, wonders or miracles, hence the frustration.

Life was really tough and finally, one night, whilst Steve was working and our baby son was fast asleep in his cot, I began to vent my frustration on

God. I was very depressed and weepy. I felt that I could not go on living like this, as I had lost all hope for the future and religion was simply not enough. I cried out to God, "Where are You Lord? I know Satan is attacking my life in so many ways, but where are You? You are supposed to be my heavenly Father and I am supposed to hear You speaking to me. I might as well have a relationship with a brick wall, and I feel as though I am going to church for a history lesson that is 2,000 years old!"

I really was desperate, and I ranted and raved at God, but then He is big enough to take it and longs for us to be real with Him. God does not want us to speak to Him with flowery religious language, especially when we are angry, hurting or frustrated on the inside. God longs for us to be real with Him, so that He can be real with us. After all, He knows what is in our heart any way. I had no idea what to expect, but I was really desperate, and I mean really desperate. Eventually I sobbed myself to sleep.

In the middle of the night I had an incredible encounter with God that has remained with me every minute of every day since then and yet is so difficult to fully explain. I will try to relate it to you.

Suddenly, God appeared on my right side, and I was standing shoulder to shoulder with Him. His presence was overwhelming and powerful, displayed by a magnificent, brilliant light, certainly not a natural light. I was overcome by an awesome love, an incredible sense of security and peace beyond words. In front of me, about three yards away, was Satan. I was not scared of him because God was standing with me. Can you believe that? The holy, awesome and magnificent God standing with me, a broken, rejected and hopeless individual! He did not wait for me to be perfect, He came to me when I was a mess and I needed Him most.

> *"The Lord delights in His people; crowning the humble with victory. Let His faithful people rejoice in this honour and sing for joy on their beds. May the praise of God be in their mouths and a double-edged sword in their hands."* Psalm 149:4-6.

God placed a huge double-edged sword into my hands. The sword was made of a shining, gleaming metal without a mark or fingerprint upon it. It was very heavy and very sharp. The sword's handle fitted perfectly in my hands as I took hold of it and the tip touched the floor. It was just the right length for me. It was as though the sword was made to measure, just for me, and although the Lord gave me no instructions, I automatically knew what to do with it.

> *"God is our shield and helper and our glorious sword. Our enemies will cower before us".* Deuteronomy 33:29

Knowing God was standing with me, I fixed my gaze upon Satan. Using all my strength, I took the sword in both hands, raising it from the floor until the tip was facing Satan. Without me speaking or taking any further action, the simple movement of raising the double-edged sword into position, caused Satan to flee immediately. I did not need to fight him or even speak to him. I simply needed to be standing where God was standing and holding my sword in position. The sword, I later discovered, represents God's powerful word.

> *"For the word of God is alive and active. Sharper than any double-edged sword, it penetrates even to dividing soul and spirit, joints and marrow; it judges the thoughts and attitudes of the heart".* Hebrews 4:12

The Lord filled me with His presence, His awesome, amazing, powerful and overwhelming peace. He then said, "I will never leave you or forsake you and I will always be there for you".

This encounter completely changed me from being hopeless, depressed and weepy – to being filled with hope, new life and unspeakable joy. I did not realise it, but I had been baptised, or some say filled, with the Holy Spirit. I discovered that God was real, and nobody could ever take that away from me. I had longed to encounter God, to hear His voice, to know

His presence and to understand how much He loved me. God met with me and I had never encountered such overwhelming love; it completely changed my life forever.

As the years unfolded since then, I came to understand the implications of what happened. The Lord put a double-edged sword in my hand, and He has been teaching me how to use it ever since. I know that God revealed Himself to me in that way because He knew what was ahead of me!

I encourage you, if you have never had an encounter with God or received the baptism of the Holy Spirit, cry out to God and ask Him to meet with you. He loves you so much and longs for you to come into His presence. Please do not settle for just a religious experience – press into God for an intimate relationship; without this we do not ever encounter the fullness of God. As Christians, it is essential for us to be filled with the Holy Spirit – without Him we are powerless.

HOW DO YOU KNOW WHAT TO FOCUS ON IF YOU WANT TO SEE BREAKTHROUGH COME?

Once again for me, my focus has come as I have fixed my eyes upon God and tried my best to listen to what He wanted me to do. I do not dream all of the time but occasionally God gives me prophetic dreams. How do I know they are not just too much cheese before I went to bed? I know because I am changed by the presence of God in those dreams and I am inspired by the direction the dream has given me.

I have not shared these dreams very often, as there are some things which you keep hidden in your heart and some people may think it is just you being boastful or arrogant. However, it may help you understand what has kept me focussed and given me direction throughout the years.

In 2002, I had a dream that I was blooming, as though I was pregnant. However, even in the dream I knew that I had had a hysterectomy and my husband Steve had had a vasectomy (just to make sure there were no more babies!) Even though I was experiencing all the symptoms of pregnancy, I was in complete denial, because I knew that it was impossible for me to conceive. I was convinced there was something wrong with me but everyone else could clearly see I was pregnant.

Just to prove everyone wrong, I carried out a pregnancy test, which was to my great shock positive. I ran in great panic to the hospital believing that, as I did not have a womb, the baby would fall out! (Please remember this was a dream!) Whilst at the hospital the midwife carried out a scan and confirmed, "Congratulations Mrs Sinclair you are pregnant!" The next day the Lord said, "You will birth in the supernatural what is impossible for you to birth in the natural".

As you can imagine I was so excited about that, although I had no comprehension of what God meant. The following night as I slept, the dream started again – just as though I was watching a television series and before the next program started, there was a little recap of the last episode.

As I slept, I picked up on the dream exactly where I had left off the night before. I was in the hospital and the midwife was carrying out a scan. She turned to me and said, "Congratulations Mrs Sinclair, you are pregnant and by the way you are having triplets!" For many years I simply had to trust God about what the triplet babies represented. Several years later the Lord showed me the triplets represented Revival, Harvest and Transformation. (A little interesting historical fact, my husband's family actually had the first surviving triplets born in Liverpool in 1939.)

This has shaped my ministry ever since, as I have focussed on Jesus and how He was going to bring these miracle babies to birth. When ministry opportunities have arisen, if they have not been looking towards bringing fruit that looks like Revival, Harvest or Transformation, I have declined the invitation.

If God gives you dreams do not let them go, even if it takes many years for them to come to fruition. Be careful who you share them with, as they are a precious gift from God for you; a gift that is all about your destiny and why God created you.

Steve and I love the film "Hidden Figures" which is the story of Katherine Johnson, born in 1918 in West Virginia, USA. Katherine was a mathematical genius but encountered many obstacles because she was a black woman. Her incredible humility, strength of character, courage and determination enabled her to bring remarkable breakthroughs for black people, for women and the NASA space race.

Another example is the story of Maria Skłodowska, born in 1867 in Warsaw, Poland. She married Pierre Curie becoming Marie Curie, the physicist and chemist who discovered Radium and Polonium. Marie Curie won two Nobel Prizes in Physics and Chemistry for her pioneering research in radioactivity. It cost Marie her life but established a tremendous medical breakthrough that we all benefit from today.

One more example of incredible breakthrough was in 1925, when the construction of the Queensway Tunnel in Liverpool began. Construction started on both sides of the River Mersey simultaneously, and without computers or the incredible machinery available today they connected within less than 25 millimetres. Some 1700 men worked on the tunnel and it cost 17 of them their lives. Breakthrough never comes in isolation, there are always people behind the scenes who have worked or prayed and paid a high price. As the two workforces dug deep under the River Mersey towards one another, there was a moment when the distance between them became so thin, it was easy to penetrate the rock and bring breakthrough. Measuring 2.1 miles, it was the longest road tunnel in the world and opened in 1934. Over the years the Queensway Tunnel changed the quality of life of thousands for people and brought revelation for tunnel construction all around the world.

We have experienced many times when God Himself came in power, to, as it were, strike the final bit of rock to bring the physical or spiritual breakthrough. However, always behind the scenes there has been a team of people on their knees crying out to God for that final shift to come that brings the breakthrough. We take no credit for the stories of extravagant breakthroughs that we share with you; we give God all the glory and thank all those behind the scenes who have done all the digging and paid the high price.

PRAYER: Thank you heavenly Father for the breakthroughs you have for me. Help me to hear your voice and to know what you are calling me to do. Amen.

Church Outside The Walls

In my first book, *Extravagant Fire*, I told the story of the poverty mindset that affected me, physically, financially and spiritually! I could never imagine that God would want to bless me and one day God really challenged me about that, and I had to repent. I believe that this was not only a huge breakthrough for me and for my family, but it was a massive breakthrough for my beloved city of Liverpool and the wider region.

The story of Liverpool Catalyst has never been told before and, up until recently, you would never have been able to find any trace of it, no website or social media page. It began in 2005 when I was asked if I would like to distribute money to Christians across Liverpool. I do not believe this would have happened, if I had not dealt with the poverty mindset that I struggled with before. The consequences when we do not press into God for our breakthrough are often so much bigger than we can understand.

The money was allocated to Christians who were not church leaders, but were serving their local communities and working with people from other churches. It was given as a gift and not a grant, in pots of no more than

£5,000 a year. I prayed about it for a millisecond and said, "I would love to help". We started small at first with two projects and grew over the years to an incredible network of amazing projects.

We called ourselves Liverpool Catalyst because a catalyst can empower activity between people, precipitating an event, change or transformation. This was exactly what we wanted to see God do, as we identified inspiring people and projects to invest the gifts into. Like me, people were overwhelmed that there were no strings attached, and that someone whom they had never met had trusted them to use the gift to make a difference in the lives of others around them.

When we started, many church leaders could not understand that members of their congregations wanted to do anything outside the church walls. If people had inspiring ideas, why could they not be used within the ministry of the church? However, God has no walls and He, like Jesus, longs to move across every sphere of our communities. Clearly, He cannot do that if we are all locked up inside our churches and only ministering within those environments. For decades, people have understood the longing for "Missionaries" to go to the nations and to share the Gospel, however most have not understood when people wanted to minister in their own communities.

We quickly discovered so many inspirational, pioneering and visionary leaders who were ministering with powerful gifting and anointing. But sadly, some were misunderstood, left unsupported and discouraged by the church. Although these people loved Jesus passionately, some had left church wounded and misjudged. What a huge loss to the Church! Thankfully, others were still very much involved with church life and really motivating others to follow in Jesus' footsteps out into the community.

We allowed Holy Spirit to lead us to people, unlike other charitable trusts who allocate funding by advertising and asking people to fill out long detailed application forms, usually with little chance of them succeeding. Holy Spirit was amazing at connecting us to the right people, at the right time; people with incredible dreams of what God could do outside the walls of the church. We had the honour of watching these projects grow and impact the lives of thousands of men, women and children across our region, nation and the world.

We remained under the radar whilst the budget we distributed grew steadily from £10,000 in 2005, to £120,000 and 179 projects in the final year of funding, distributing £1.6 million over all those years. Personally, I was overwhelmed that someone I had never met, trusted me to do this on their behalf. I was also very humbled by the opportunity and impacted by the incredible people we encountered. Liverpool Catalyst developed to much more than a mechanism of distributing funds, it became a group of like-minded people, supporting each other and working to make a difference in order to see God's kingdom come across Liverpool.

We even hosted "Angel's Dens" which were opportunities for people to come and present their ideas to us and we would do our best to help them. Jacqui came to one of those with Jennie who led "Celebrate Recovery". Jacqui looked so much older than she was, but as she shared her story and impacted our hearts so powerfully, we understood why. Jacqui was in recovery after a horrific life of drug and alcohol addiction leading her into the sex worker industry.

Jacqui had us all in tears as she told us how she had been sexually abused, often climbing into cars with men and not knowing if she would be killed that night. She had been raped and gang raped, many times at knife point. Jacqui was battered and broken until she met Jesus through Jennie. Jacqui got clean and became a part of the team helping others. We were so proud of all that she had achieved, especially a few nights later when we were guests at the Launch Night for Celebrate Recovery. Jacqui stood in front of so many people and shared her story with great humility and vulnerability.

It was a very powerful night and many people signed up to be part of the next Celebrate Recovery course.

Tragically, a few weeks later, we were heartbroken to hear that Jacqui had died. We attended her funeral, led so beautifully by Jennie and their vicar. Money was raised to do something in honour of Jacqui, and to help other vulnerable women. Jacqui had a dream that one day some of the sex workers would tell their stories at the Everyman Theatre, to help others understand the horror and the trauma of their lives. We were invited to see the girls do exactly that a few months later, and, although they were really nervous, it was a very powerful production and left everyone in floods of tears. We were all devastated that anyone should go through what they go through almost every day. Jacqui's dream came to pass, and these precious women all gave their lives to Jesus.

One girl's story was horrific and she was so emaciated she could hardly stand up! I was pleased to hear that Jennie managed to get this precious woman into a Rehabilitation Centre. A year later this beautiful woman came to me, totally transformed by Jesus' love, as He had set her free from the drug addiction. Praise God!!

There are many stories of lives totally changed by God's love through the various projects. From people with addictions, to arts and dramas helping people out of isolation and depression. Hundreds of children, young people and their families have been helped by the school projects. People helped with incredible projects working within the prisons and with the prisoners' families. We also had two wonderful projects aimed at preventing domestic violence and helping people escape from it safely.

We saw the rise of Street Pastor's Teams right across our region, helping the night-time economies become so much safer. Sadly too, we saw the increase of Food Banks in every area of our region. How dreadful that in this century, people in our communities are going hungry! I have not even mentioned the many projects working with the homeless or those working with refugees. We are thrilled to continue seeing hundreds of Muslims encountering Jesus' life-transforming love, and I was overwhelmed to be personally invited to help with their baptisms.

We recognised and supported leaders by hosting training and networking days. This gave leaders the opportunity to hear and learn from each other's successes, struggles and failures. Working together with other projects drew leaders from working in isolation and gave them a network of people with shared beliefs and goals they could connect with. Liverpool Catalyst provided an opportunity for people to be empowered to live in unity, to fulfil their destinies, and to see their dreams come to fruition. We all had a heart to see many lives and our region transformed by Jesus' love.

MIRACLES RELEASED

During one of our networking days we asked some of our leaders a specific question. "What do you need the most right now?" Pastor Roy Farrell from Victory Outreach told us how they had a home for men where they could get help to recover from drug or alcohol abuse. However, they had many women desperate for help too, but no home for women. I asked everyone there, "Do you think that God thinks this is important?" Everyone replied, "Yes". "Do you think that God can provide for this home?" Once again everyone replied, "Yes". "Ok let us stand together and stretch our hands towards Roy and pray a prayer of agreement and release this house from heaven." So, we all stood together and stretched out our hands in Roy's direction and we prayed, thanking God for this house.

Claire shared about her work with "YKids", an incredible children and youth project. We asked her the same question. "What do you need the most right now?" Claire explained how they had to give their staff redundancy notices because they were desperately short of funds. Again, I asked everyone, "Do you think that God thinks this is important?" Everyone replied, “Yes”. “Do you think that God can provide for this work?” Once again everyone replied, “Yes”. “Ok let us stand together and stretch our hands towards Claire and we will pray a prayer of agreement and release this money from heaven.”

We have an amazing God who loves His people and is so good at bringing incredible breakthroughs and this was one of those days. One hour later, Roy slipped into the empty seat next to me. He told me he had just received a call from someone offering to buy them a ten-bedroom house for the women. Now that house is a home full of women being set free from drug and alcohol addictions. Praise God!

I received a call from Claire a few hours later the same day and she was excited to tell me, that they had checked their bank account and discovered they had received a surprise donation of £50,000.

There is breakthrough power released because of our heavenly Father’s pleasure when His people truly stand in unity together. There was real momentum, as God’s love was being shared and groups supported and helped one another. Food Banks shared their food if they had too much whilst others Food Banks were short of stock. Groups served one another for the greater good – that is what the kingdom looks like.

Early 2019, the funding ended as the charitable trust providing the resources closed. Pam and I had felt really devastated at the thought that this should close when God’s fingerprints were so clearly all over it. We knew that Liverpool Catalyst was always more than the distribution of money and so we asked God what He wanted us to do next.

Shift of season

What happened next took us all by surprise! We met some of the leaders we had been working with for many years and explained everything. They unanimously agreed they would step up to help us. So that day a new team was created, and we appointed Community Champions for Addictions, Children and Youth, Community Transformation, Creative Arts, Families, Prisons, Homeless, Poverty, Prisons, Sex Workers, Refugees and Muslims and Regeneration.

We established goals to help mobilise churches, organisations and individuals in their mission to serve our city region and to facilitate partnerships between them for everyone's benefit. We explored how we could encourage new initiatives that met local needs and provide opportunities for training, networking and support for those leading projects. We empowered our Community Champions to share their diverse wealth of experience and wisdom with others in the region. We shared stories because we knew it was important to enable the bigger picture of what God was doing across our region to be seen. We encouraged prayer that changes lives, celebrating our successes and standing together when times were hard. Lastly, we set up a website and Facebook page providing lots of funding information and a place for everyone to connect.

Someone gave us a generous financial gift and encouraged us to host an amazing thanksgiving celebration, for all that had been achieved in the past and to launch for the new season.

Days later, on 29th April 2019, God spoke through a dream, showing me Stanley Dock in Liverpool. Humpback whales were tossing in the water giving us an incredible display and people were coming from miles around to see them. God spoke clearly to me and said, "Liverpool will be a place of incredible signs, wonders and miracles. All we need to do is keep giving God the glory!"

I researched and discovered we had never had humpback whales of any kind in Liverpool. However, exactly one month later, humpback whales were projected on to a huge fountain of water in one of the Liverpool docks for five nights, as part of the spectacular River Festival. Thousands of people came to watch these incredible shows. We knew it was a sign confirming the dream the Lord had given me.

Not only am I the Director of Liverpool Catalyst but I am also the Director and Founder of the Community Watchmen Ministries (CWM) Team. This is a team of Christians from all denominations across Liverpool and the wider region. We all love Jesus, believe in the power of prayer and the importance of the prophetic gifts. A few days after the dream, our CWM Team arranged to go on a prayer tour of Liverpool. We sailed on the Mersey Ferry where we prayed for twelve anaesthetists from Cairo, who happened to be taking some time out from a medical conference they were attending in Liverpool. We prayed for our city and region as we sailed up and down the River Mersey. We followed that up with a bus tour of the city, praying around the city and jumping off at strategic places like the Cathedrals (we have two in Liverpool – one for the Catholics and one for the Church of England). We decided to end our Prayer Tour by visiting Stanley Dock, the site of the dream.

After further research, I discovered the surrounding area was the largest regeneration project of its kind in Europe and the work was being led by Harcourt Developments. Their website was another incredible encouragement to us as their strapline for this particular project was "Dream Big".

The beautiful Titanic Hotel is located on the side of Stanley Dock, at the end of the Leeds to Liverpool Canal and opposite the huge regeneration project. So, we finished our prayer tour there with refreshments and more prayer. It was easy to see this was the venue we needed to host our Celebration.

Pam and I returned to the Titanic Hotel after a phone call enquiring about the availability and cost of hosting a dinner for 170 people. Despite being told the room we needed was not available, we knew this was the venue God had hand-picked for our Celebration. The young lady explained that the Rum Warehouse function room was already booked, but when we asked her, she took us to view it. I said, "No this is not the room – do you have another one available?" She led us to the opposite end of the Hotel, to West Bay which had a private reception and bar area. This was perfect and we knew it was our venue! We asked about the price, and she kindly said, "Sorry it is above your budget". She disappeared to double check availability and I whispered to Pam, "We will book this because either the Lord will provide the extra money, or the Titanic Hotel will reduce the price!"

We waited in anticipation and she returned a few minutes later with a big smile. "I have managed to find an alternative menu which will bring the dinner within your budget." Praise the Lord! Breakthrough! We quickly drew up our guest list, sent out the invitations, started making beautiful favours, goody bags and decorations for the tables. We arranged the program, the after-dinner speaker, Ian Yates came to lead worship, and we had an incredible surprise from a large store who provided us with gifts for each of the Project Leaders.

A few days before our celebration, Harcourt Developments who owned the 1.8 million sq. ft of Liverpool's historic docks including the Tobacco Warehouse (the largest brick-built building in the world), installed brightly lit, large bill-board size signage at either end of the dock. What did they say? "DREAM BIG". God was speaking for sure!

Our celebration was a wonderful evening of giving thanks to God for the past, telling some of the inspiring stories, networking and listening to one another. Suddenly, during the time of worship, all the power popped and the whole atmosphere was filled with God's presence as we glorified Him. There was such a sense of excitement, as everyone recognised that God was doing something very special. Now we await the signs, wonders and more miracles, and we give the Lord all the glory, as we dream bigger dreams!

> *"Never doubt God's mighty power to work in you and accomplish all this. He will achieve infinitely more than your greatest request, your most unbelievable dream, and exceed your wildest imagination! He will outdo them all, for his miraculous power constantly energizes you. Now we offer up to God all the glorious praise that rises from every church in every generation through Jesus Christ-and all that will yet be manifest through time and eternity. Amen!"* Ephesians 3:20-21 (TPT)

Since then we have launched our Facebook page and website www.liverpoolcatalyst.com with lots of information about the projects, funding opportunities and so much more.

PRAYER: Help me heavenly Father to see where I can help or serve you in my community physically, prayerfully or financially. Amen.

ONE STEP AT A TIME

SOUTH AFRICA 2015

Before I share the story of our trips to the nations where we experienced so many breakthroughs, I want to encourage you that these journeys always start with the first little steps. Like a baby needs to learn to roll, before it learns to crawl, before it learns to stand, before it learns to walk, before it learns to run.

For us, our first step was praying about the transatlantic slave trade and its impact upon Liverpool. At the end of 1999 Liverpool issued an apology. Next, we were invited to go to Berlin to represent Liverpool and the UK to remember and repent for the way that the European nations had carved up Africa at the Berlin Conference of 1884. This was our second and very painful step, as we recognised the horrendous sins of our nations and repented on behalf of the UK and then the African nations released forgiveness to us.

Then God released authority to us to actually engage with Africa, the third step. We had repented for the sin of our city and then God spoke clearly to us that we should no longer repent, as He had forgiven us, but now we (The CWM Team) needed to sow life. So, we began to raise funds and committed ourselves to partner with Arnold Muwonge in Uganda, to build a home for children as part of the Kampala Children's Centre. However, it did not end there, we then knew that God was calling us to GO! Now that was a huge step of faith and I personally would not have gone except that I knew God was calling me to go! You need to read the story in *Extravagant Adventures* as we experienced a massive breakthrough and because of our obedience, Uganda experienced God's extravagant breakthrough.

God just kept increasing the steps from Uganda, to South Africa, to Rwanda and then on to Ghana with many nations in between. Each time we took a step of faith, God increased the anointing, the favour, the authority and the breakthroughs. It is extremely humbling as we are just a little team of people based in Liverpool who are pursuing God for healing, transformation, harvest and revival. We give Jesus the glory because nothing would have happened without His influence.

Personal and community breakthroughs came during our second trip to South Africa in 2015. It started just before we flew to South Africa – the Cecil Rhodes Memorial Statue located at the front of the Cape Town University was removed. The students had taken a vote after ongoing protests about the British Coloniser and it was taken down! Exactly a year earlier we had prayed with Councillor Gerald Siljeur at the Cecil Rhodes Memorial built into the side of Table Mountain. There was an inscription below the bust of Cecil Rhodes which had the last four lines from the 1902 poem "Burial" by Rudyard Kipling in honour of Rhodes: "The immense and brooding spirit still shall quicken and control. Living he was the land, and dead, His soul shall be her soul!"

We knew this was controlling the nation even from the grave and it needed to be broken. We had prayed prayers of repentance on behalf of the British, who through Cecil Rhodes had not only done many good things but had caused great damage through manipulation and control of this beautiful nation and others. We held hands with Councillor Gerald Siljeur and with deep sorrow, we stood in the gap on behalf of the British and asked for forgiveness. It was a very powerful time and we knew God had heard our prayers. It was encouraging for us to hear that even before we landed back in South Africa, God was moving, and the removal of the Cape Town university statue was a dramatic sign of that to us.

All you need Is love

Norma Dean, Steve and I were kept very busy ministering in churches on our first Sunday. We were welcomed by lovely congregations who were so hungry for God and God kept us busy ministering to them. Later that day, the Kingdom Ministries International (KMI) Conference began at Engedi Church in Mitchell's Plain. I spoke about the difference between being an orphan and living as a child of God. The whole thing about our identity is critical if we are going to be vessels to bring heaven to earth.

Last time we visited South Africa, we had hoped to visit Table Mountain, but we never quite made it. Thankfully, this time we were able to and there was a cable car lift that revolves 360 degrees internally, giving you an amazing view as you ascend and descend. We walked around the top, which was almost flat and prayed at places that gave a clear view over Cape Town. In one place we stopped to sing, "All you need is Love" (a great song from the Beatles) over Cape Town and South Africa. It was such a blessing when other people including a couple of the Reserve Rangers joined in with the singing. What fun, but also what a prophetic message to be released!

During the next session at Engedi Church we prayed for a fresh infilling of the Holy Spirit and fresh anointing for the intercessors and prophets. We put people into groups to identify the major issues in their community, with a view to us preparing a prayer strategy with them, so they could begin to pray effectively and really see some breakthroughs come.

We shared the following prophetic word the Lord had given to us for South Africa:

> "There has been a SHIFT in your nation as the statue of Cecil Rhodes has been removed, as a sign to you that what has been controlling you in the past is being removed. However, just like when a house is swept clean, if the Holy Spirit does not occupy the house then the demonic will return with greater power. God is saying you need to walk free from the orphan spirit and take hold of your destinies as God's children, to rule and reign in power over the land the Lord has given you."

> *'When an impure spirit comes out of a person, it goes through arid places seeking rest and does not find it. Then it says, "I will return to the house I left". When it arrives, it finds the house unoccupied, swept clean and put in order. Then it goes and takes with it seven other spirits more wicked than itself, and they go in and live there. And the final condition of that person is worse than the first. That is how it will be with this wicked generation.'* Matthew 12:43-45

We placed a white line across the front of the church, and invited people to step up to the line as a sign that they were willing to stand in the gap to see heaven come to earth for Mitchell's Plain. Everyone came to make a fresh commitment to God and then we asked if they wanted to stand for Cape Town to take a further step forward, and then once again we prayed. Finally, we asked people to step forward again if they wanted to stand for the nation of South Africa. We felt there was a real breakthrough as people committed themselves to be vessels of change, breakthrough and blessing.

The weight of God's presence

One breakthrough in particular came when an amazing lady called Mama Thandi arrived. We had never met her before, so we did not know that she was against Christians falling on the floor when they are being prayed for. We also did not know that Mama Thandi did not agree with Christians being anointed with oil. However, at the end of the evening whilst Holy Spirit was moving very powerfully, we laid hands on Mama Thandi and the weight of God's presence fell heavily upon her. Thankfully, a couple of men were there to catch her and gently lower her to the floor because she was incapable of standing up on her own. Mama Thandi was having an incredible encounter with God there on the floor and whilst there, as with everyone else, we anointed her with oil as a sign of the fresh commissioning that God was releasing. Thankfully, we were listening to God and doing what He told us to do and that released a massive breakthrough for Mama Thandi. God was touching her so much that she was still on the floor when we left the building over half an hour later! Often you never get to hear what God has done, but a year later we were blessed when we began to hear about the breakthroughs she had experienced.

Over twenty years ago, when I was really struggling with no self-esteem or confidence, and I was suffering from Post-Traumatic Stress Disorder, two men prophesied over me. They told me that God was opening doors for me to go into Parliaments, Governments and Nations to bring God's word and to release breakthroughs. It was a moment in my life when I certainly thought that was impossible. However, many years later thanks to God's work in my life, going through these doors has become normal for me.

The next day, we visited the South African Parliament again with Counsellor Gerald Siljeur, Steve Swart MP, Gary and Cheryl Smythe, Jacqui Schmidt, and Latasha and Mario Greenwood. Steve Swart gave us a special guided tour of the area including the different Parliamentary buildings. We presented Steve Swart and Gerald Siljeur with keys and they were really overwhelmed and overjoyed as God had been speaking to Steve about keys. Two days later, South Africa celebrated "Freedom Day" and twenty-one years since the liberation of their country and people from a long period of colonialism and white minority domination known as apartheid. In both Britain and South Africa, we celebrate 21st birthdays by giving keys, so our keys were significant.

Signs and wonders

Friday evening, we started the Conference at New Life Vineyard Church. Norma spoke on "The Shift" including what happens when tectonic plates begin to move. Incredibly and shockingly, the following morning at 11.56am in Nepal there was a 7.8 magnitude earthquake that killed at least 7,000 people and injured at least twice as many. The earthquake also caused a huge avalanche on Everest, which destroyed the base camp and killed a further nineteen people. When things begin to SHIFT it's not always nice, but we need to be ready to align ourselves with what God is doing in the midst of the changing seasons!

The next day, our little team ministered in Pastor Chris Slosters' church, The Revival Centre in Mitchell's Plain. We were thrilled to have so many church leaders there from across the region. I spoke on "The Transfiguration" and then we had a very powerful ministry time as we encouraged the leaders to actually pray and bless one another. As they began to pray for one another you could feel the whole atmosphere change as God came! What a time of blessing!

The following day was Freedom Day and the 21st Anniversary for this beautiful nation. We were thrilled to attend the Youth Transformation Prayer Gathering at the Newlands Rugby Stadium. It was fabulous to be with so many young people loving on Jesus. Angus Buchan was the main speaker and was so powerful – a good old fashioned straight down the line fiery preacher. Angus preached the Gospel and asked people to stand if they were giving their lives to Jesus and almost everybody in the Stadium stood just to make sure.

On Tuesday, we met Jan and Wendy Slabbert, and leaders from across Wellington and Paarl who had never met together before. I shared the story of what God is doing and the transformation we had begun to see in Liverpool. I also shared that I had recently watched Selma – the story of

Martin Luther King who had a vision to be a pastor in a little church, with occasional speaking engagements and a nice little home for his family! God had other plans! God has bigger Kingdom plans for the Church of Wellington and Paarl.

We had an amazing response from everyone and spent lots of time ministering to them all. One pastor had his seven-year-old son with him who was almost completely deaf. One ear was entirely deaf, and the other had only slight hearing with the help of a hearing aid. Norma prayed for him three times and the third time this little boy began to hear! Praise the Lord!

In the evening we ministered at "Tell Them Ministries", a church led by Pastor Peter John in Mitchell's Plain. Peter John is a very humble man and a very gifted evangelist with a huge heart. He leads thousands of people to Jesus during his missions in Pakistan and actually just that morning had led over fifty people to Jesus whilst on the train to Cape Town! I interviewed Peter and asked him how many people he led to Jesus the first time he preached the Gospel on the trains. He replied, "Nobody". So, I asked him, "How long did it take before you saw anyone respond to the Gospel?" He replied, "Over five years, but I knew God had called me to this ministry, so I never gave up until the breakthrough came". Now he sees people saved every day!

Once again, during the ministry time, God moved very powerfully as we prayed for everyone. A real spirit of joy fell, and I found it almost impossible to pray for anyone as it hit me too! So often when the Holy Spirit is around, I am filled with God's gift of joy. In Galatians 5:22-23 Paul wrote:

> *"The fruit of the Spirit is love, joy, peace, forbearance, kindness, goodness, faithfulness, gentleness and self-control".*

We spent time praying for the five office gifts of the church. Llewellyn represented the Apostolic, Peter the Evangelist, Mario the Prophet and two others represented the Teacher and the Pastor. Seeing these five precious men from different churches standing together was so powerful and you could see mindsets shifting to make way for Kingdom thinking. Since Peter has such a powerful anointing for evangelism, we asked him to pray for us too.

We had a surprise visit from Pastor Daniel Klienbooi who we had met last year when we visited Steve Swart MP in Parliament. I had prophesied over him saying that God was going to use him greatly in the Parliament and that he would be a father figure to many. Daniel had written to me, "When you were speaking, tears of joy were flowing down my face because I really began to understand a prophetic word that was given to me back in 2007. I am now convinced more than ever that God wants me in Parliament, ministering to the political leadership of the country".

Since our last time with Daniel, they had released the church to someone else and sold their home. His wife Maria had transferred her job to Cape Town and now they were looking for a new home. We had an exciting time with them listening to how God was unfolding His plans. I knew that Daniel was going to make a significant difference in Parliament, and we looked forward to meeting up with him again soon. I love divine appointments and it is so brilliant to see what God is doing.

What a time we had – divine appointments, personal breakthroughs, community breakthroughs, shifts and lives changed. God was truly amazing, and we give Him all the glory for the foundations laid for our next visit.

PRAYER: Heavenly Father I pray that you will guide me, so that I can take the right steps to position myself, so that I am in the right place, at the right time, with the right people, doing the right thing for heaven to come to earth. Amen.

Partnerships For Breakthrough

South Africa 2016

Norma and I flew out to South Africa once again in 2016, with a sense this was going to be a very powerful time, as the Lord was going to kick-start transformation. On our first morning, we were thrilled to go with Gary and Cheryl Smythe, to a meeting with Ray Wilson, who had a really big heart for God and for community transformation. Ray organised a meeting and invited lots of the senior Bishops and church leaders from Khayelitsha. This is a huge township, notorious for seriously high crime and over half of Cape Town's unemployed live in this area. In the natural it would be a frightening place to go, but because we knew God wanted us there, we knew we would be safe. The important thing is to be in the right place, at the right time, with the right people, doing the right thing and that allows you to be a vessel to bring heaven to earth.

We were pleased that General Brandt, the equivalent of our Police Chief Superintendent, was attending. The biggest surprise was to see the local Imam in the midst of around eighty Christian leaders. Many of the leaders there were looking to the police to provide finances for their church projects, including a request for funding to enable the churches to host Alpha courses. I was shocked that the church would expect the police to pay for their Alpha courses and yet had no sense of care for the police and the awful job they had to do in their communities.

There was a lot of talk before General Brandt, with great humility, spoke simply but powerfully, sharing a poem written by someone in the South African Police Service.

"I have pulled dead, mangled bodies from cars. I have lied to people as they were dying. I said you are going to be fine as I held their hand and watched the life fade out. I have picked up dead unwanted babies from dustbins. Struggled to keep my pose while I pick up rotten and decomposed bodies, attempting to keep my sanity by making jokes about it.

Bought lunch for people who were mentally ill and haven't eaten in a while. I have had people try to stab me. Fought with men trying to shoot me. Been attacked by women who were badly beaten by their husband as I was arresting him.

I have held towels on bullet wounds. Done CPR when I knew it wouldn't help, just to make family members feel better. I have broken down doors, fought in drug houses. Chased fugitives though the streets.

I have been in high speed car chases. Foot chases across the township during rush hour traffic. Had to calm down large angry crowds by myself. Drove like a mad person to help a fellow officer or a public member in need of help. Let little kids, who don't have much, sit in my police vehicle and pretend they are a cop for their birthday.

I have taken a lot of people to jail. Prayed for people I don't even know. Yes, and at times, I have been violent when I had to be. I have been kind when I could.

I admit I have drove to some dark place and cried by myself when I was overwhelmed. I have missed Christmas and other holidays with my family more than I wanted too. Every cop I know has done all these things and more for a lousy pay, long hours and a short life expectancy.

We don't want your pity; I don't care for your respect. Just let us do our jobs and to serve the people of this country, without killing us."

I was so emotional after listening to General Brandt and full of sorrow for the situation described in the poem. How on earth was I going to speak? A few moments later, I was introduced and I began by reading 1 Timothy 2:1-4:

> *"I urge, then, first of all, that petitions, prayers, intercession and thanksgiving be made for all people – for Kings and all those in authority, that we may live peaceful and quiet lives in all godliness and holiness. This is good, and pleases God our Saviour, who wants all people to be saved and to come to a knowledge of the truth."*

I then turned to General Brandt and with great sorrow, repented on behalf of the church, that we had not been obedient to the word of God by praying for him and his officers. We had left them vulnerable, because as the church we had not been praying for their protection and we had not honoured or appreciated them. General Brandt and many leaders were fighting back the tears as the Holy Spirit was powerfully moving across the room. This was a time of revelation and breakthrough for the church, who came to ask for money, but God turned the tables on them!

I shared some of the story of how Jesus had been answering our prayers to transform our beloved City of Liverpool, from the drug distribution capital of the UK in 2002, to the Entrepreneurial Capital (February 2016). The Talk Business Magazine reported, "The population of Liverpool is estimated at 440,000 with 134,569 new companies starting over the past two years. This results in an entrepreneurial population percentage of 16%. Birmingham's was 14.5% followed closely by Manchester 14%. These numbers are significantly higher than the UK average 2% and London's just 7.5%."[3] That is a massive breakthrough! Praise God!

This was clearly a time of awakening, as there was now a desperate desire amongst the church leaders and police to see God move in this community and across Cape Town too. Crime and violence had been rampaging out of control in many areas for far too long, because of poverty and hopelessness. It was good to hear that these leaders appeared to be ready to do whatever God wanted to see transformation happen. There was a great response and an eagerness to meet again before we returned to England.

Throwing down a challenge

Before we left the meeting, we were introduced to Mama Thandi and she told us the story of what had happened since the last time we had met. Thandi leads a group of precious older ladies called The Annas (in remembrance of the Prophetess Anna who waited in the temple until she saw baby Jesus). The Annas were intercessors and God was about to give them a challenge! I had the joy of introducing Thandi to General Brandt and we chatted for a little while before I asked General Brandt to give Thandi and the Annas two of their worst cases that they had been struggling to solve. We left them in deep conversation and waited to hear of the incredible breakthroughs that came from this encounter.

Do not be afraid to reach out with a word of encouragement to someone when God gives you a nudge. It is important to have some time off to relax and recharge your batteries, but never switch them off! Wherever we went, God was giving us words to bless people, because wherever you go people are waiting to encounter Jesus.

---

3. "Liverpool is the UK's most entrepreneurial city of 2015", *Talk Business*. https://www.talk-business.co.uk/2016/02/26/14356/

We were ready for an early night with our host Penny, however God had arranged a divine appointment. Michael and Pete arrived (names have been changed) in quite a state; Pete was sobbing, distressed, angry and heartbroken. He had recently discovered that his wife had not only had an affair, but their youngest child was not his. Pete was struggling desperately to find a way forward, as he adored this child who he now discovered had been fathered by another man.

As we prayed for him, we asked Father God to fill him with peace and he began to calm down. Praise God it was not long before Pete gave his life to Jesus and he was filled with God's love and joy, leaving us with a huge smile on his face. Michael poured out his heart too, previously he had a chaotic life taking drugs and as a result his wife had turned to other men, conceiving two children to two of them. However, Michael found Jesus, he made a good choice to come off the drugs and was now bringing up their children, including the two who he had not fathered. Tragically, his wife had long since gone and was selling her body on the streets.

So much for our quiet night but it was a very powerful night. I was deeply touched by these two fathers and reminded of Malachi 4:5-6 *"See, I will send you the prophet Elijah to you before that great and dreadful day of the LORD comes. He will turn the hearts of the parents to their children, and the hearts of the children to their parents; or else I will come and strike the land with total destruction".* After they left, we had a very powerful time in God's presence giving thanks for all He had done.

The following evening we were at Engedi Church, meeting with the intercessors and sharing from the Community Transformation Prayer Strategy, written following our time with them last year. We unpacked the section on gangs and drugs, before we spent some time coaching them in prophetic prayer. They quickly got the idea as they are great intercessors and we watched as they began to put it all into practice.

Tuesday we were taken by Pastor Jonathan Naicker, Alfie and Lena Fabe for a wonderful tour of the Cape of Good Hope where the Indian and Atlantic Oceans meet. This is the southernmost tip of Africa and it was important for us to be there to pray for the whole of Africa.

Gunfights and dead bodies

I was driven to Jesus Connection Church (JCC) located in the very poor coloured community of Eastridge in Mitchell's Plain on Wednesday evening. As we arrived, there seemed to be a lot of people hanging about and tensions were running very high. I stepped out of the car, fixed my eyes on the door and walked calmly straight into the church.

Pastor Jonathan asked if we had experienced any trouble getting through to the church. I told him we simply walked straight through the middle of the crowd! Jonathan looked surprised, as he told us the shocking news that two of the biggest and most violent local gangs – the Americans and the 28s (the 28s are recruited from the Prison Wing 28) had just had a "shoot out" on the field just across the road from the church. At least five people were killed and perhaps up to eight! Apparently, some of their bodies were still lying in the road and we had just walked right through the middle of it all! Again, the importance of being in the right place, at the right time, with the right people, doing the right thing is crucial. A few minutes earlier and we could have been killed!

Life seemed so cheap here! I was shocked that people did not seem to know or care how many men had been killed. To me that was really important as they were all somebody's son and their parents would be broken-hearted. I was told that their bodies would be dragged away, ahead of the police arriving and quickly buried before the end of the day according to Muslim tradition.

With great sadness in my heart, we began to worship Jesus and to enthrone him afresh in the Eastridge community. The children in the choir were singing, almost immune to what had just happened. It was a beautiful sight to see them oblivious to what was going on around them and simply lost in worshipping Jesus! Apparently, most of them came from very broken families, many without fathers and some in families struggling with all kinds of addictions. Thankfully, you could clearly see JCC is a place where they are loved, secure, happy and fed spiritually, and in their stomachs too!

I taught on "Praying on site with insight" which was powerful and very relevant, as we planned to pray in the area where the gangs meet on Saturday morning. The next chapter contains a snippet of the teaching which may help you understand what we did and what you can do, when you pray in your community.

PRAYER: Heavenly Father I ask you to guide me so that I am able to meet and partner with the right people, at the right time so that we can be vessels to bring heaven to earth wherever you lead us. Amen.

Praying On Site With Insight

South Africa 2016

"Because Jesus lives forever, he has a permanent priesthood. Therefore, he is able to save completely those who come to God through him, because he always lives to intercede for them". Hebrews 7:24-26

The Bible tells us that Jesus ever lives to intercede. Clearly if Jesus considers intercession is really important – so should we! Intercession is talking to God about the people rather than talking to the people about God. God said to Jeremiah *"Call to me and I will answer you and tell you great and mighty things, which you do not know"* Jeremiah 33:3 (NKJV). If Jesus ever lives to intercede, what is Jesus praying for you, for your family, for your community and for your nation?

Praying on site with insight is such a powerful way of praying in our communities, because it becomes a seeing, hearing, touching and smelling experience. It uses all our natural senses, as well as our spiritual gifts, helped by our understanding of some of the history of the land.

Matthew 28:18-19 says *"Jesus came to them and said, 'All authority in heaven and on earth has been given to me. Therefore go.'"* God releases His power as we walk and talk with Him. We walk in humility and not arrogance or pride to help us to avoid being judgmental about what we see, as that will affect how we pray.

We prayer walk or drive or cycle etc. in the authority of Jesus, not in our own authority and not to bring condemnation as in Luke 10:1-20 and Romans 8:34. We walk with the Holy Spirit, listening to Him, allowing Him to guide us and encourage us to pray what is on God's heart.

> *"In the same way, the Spirit helps us in our weakness. We do not know what we ought to pray for, but the Spirit himself intercedes for us through wordless groans".* Romans 8:26

Not only can we listen and be led by our heavenly Father, but if we are filled with the Holy Spirit then we are able to release His love and power out into the places and people we are praying for. Remember, you are an Ambassador for Christ – one who represents the King of another Kingdom.

> *"We are therefore Christ's Ambassadors, as though God were making his appeal through us. We implore you on Christ's behalf: Be reconciled to God".* 2 Corinthians 5:20

You need to be spiritually and practically prepared and the question is how do you do that? Do some research about the place where you are going to pray. What is its history, what is it currently used for and are there any plans for the future? You can do this via the newspapers and the internet. What are the positive and negative things about the place?

A great Biblical example is when Moses reached the edge of the Promised Land and God told him to send spies into the land.

> *"Go up through the Negev and on into the hill country. See what the land is like and whether the people who live there are strong or weak,*

few or many. What kind of land do they live in? Is it good or bad? What kind of towns do they live in? Are they unwalled or fortified? How is the soil? Is it fertile or poor? Are there trees on it or not?" Numbers 13:17-20.

Joshua 2:1 tells us that Joshua did the same when he took over from Moses. "Joshua secretly sent two spies to go look over the land". Also, Joshua 18:4 *"Appoint three men from each tribe, I will send them out to make a survey of the land and to write a description of it".*

History and geography are important for us to understand if we want to see the land cleansed and healed.

- Why was your town or city formed and who founded it?
- Where did the money come from?
- What happened there good or bad e.g. murders, revivals?
- Where are the gateways and communication networks?
- What significant buildings are there e.g. churches, places of false religions, etc?

There are many reasons why the land may need to be healed or cleansed:

1) Oppression – Where people have been governed harshly or treated with cruelty or injustice. *"Therefore you shall not oppress one another, but you shall fear the Lord your God".* Leviticus 25:17 (NKJV)

2) Idolatry and pride – anything that takes the place of God in our lives. *"I will repay them double for their wickedness and their sin, because they have defiled my land with the lifeless forms of their vile images and have filled my inheritance with their detestable idols".* Jeremiah 16:18

3) Bloodshed – Murder, abortion, grievous bodily harm, assault, violence and blood pacts. *"Cain said to his brother Abel, 'Let's go out to the*

field.' While they were in the field, Cain attacked his brother Abel and killed him. Then the Lord said to Cain, 'Where is your brother Abel?' 'I don't know,' he replied. 'Am I my brother's keeper?' The Lord said, 'What have you done? Listen! Your brother's blood cries out to me from the ground. Now you are under a curse and driven from the ground, which opened its mouth to receive your brother's blood from your hand.'" Genesis 4:8-10

4) Sexual immorality – read Leviticus 18:6-30.

It is important to be prepared practically as well as spiritually. Wear comfortable, culturally acceptable clothing and footwear. Pray together as a team prior to the beginning of the walk and if you can, take communion. If you are going to pray with others, try to walk in small groups of two or three so you do not look too obvious. Always pray in unity with one another and pray with your eyes open, so you can be sensitive to what you see that might prompt prayer. Continue to listen and talk with God, as you pray and use scriptures in your prayers. Do not forget to smile at people you meet. God may be working in their life and you may have an opportunity to pray for them.

Pray in co-operation with people who are already ministering in that area – you are there to support what God is already doing there. Be flexible as the Holy Spirit leads and pray together as a team at the end of the walk. Keep a journal at the conclusion and watch for the answers to your prayers.

There are two main categories of prayer walking:

Regular prayer walking around your community. Wherever you are walking you can pray – on your way to the shops, school or church. Releasing the blessing of God simply walking and coming in the opposite spirit of anything negative you see:

- Poverty – release provision.
- Death – release life.
- Violence – release peace.
- Isolation – release friendship.
- Poor education – release a hunger to learn.
- Ill health – release health of spirit, soul and mind.

a. Pray for: homes, schools, colleges and universities, businesses, local councils and places of government, hospitals, police and churches plus however God leads.

b. Pray blessing over:
   - Body – health, protection, strength
   - Labour – work, income, security
   - Emotional – joy, peace, hope
   - Social – love, marriage, family, friends
   - Spiritual – salvation, faith, grace

Specific prayer assignments when God speaks to you about a particular place. This could be when you have to travel to a location as a team e.g. Washington DC, Windsor Castle, Westminster and in this case Eastridge in South Africa.

There are some safety guidelines we would encourage you to use: DO NOT TAKE ON THE DEMONIC AS YOU ARE PRAYER WALKING – e.g. If you see signs of a spirit of death in operation or freemasonry etc. do not start binding these principalities. Talk to God about them – ask God why they are there and then deal with the root sin that has given them permission to function there. For example, we started with God showing us there was a spirit of death over Liverpool so we asked God, "Why did it have permission to be there?" This was when God began to speak to us about the sin of the transatlantic slave trade which was our first step.

Pray in the armour of God – *"truth, righteousness, peace, faith, salvation, and the Word of God with prayer and petition pray at all times in the Spirit . . ."* Ephesians 6:14-18.

God is looking for those who will stand in the gap to see our cities and communities cleansed and healed. He is looking for those who have faith to believe that God can do it! We need to spend time worshipping Jesus, pausing to listen and walk in obedience with Him, giving God the glory for all He does. I hope this helps as you look at your community.

Praying on site in Eastridge

It is hard to begin to describe what happened that Saturday morning, but it was time to see a breakthrough! Many people quote:

> *"When I shut up the heavens so that there is no rain, or command locusts to devour the land or send a plague among my people, if my people, who are called by my name, will humble themselves and pray and seek my face and turn from their wicked ways, then will I hear from heaven and will forgive their sin and will heal their land. Now my eyes will be open and my ears attentive to the prayers offered in this place".* 2 Chronicles 7:13-15

But so few people are actually willing to truly humble themselves, and certainly not so concerned or have the hope to believe that they can see their land transformed or healed. This particular morning in Eastridge though, we participated in something very special.

We gathered at 9am at JCC Church and I was very glad to have Norma, Gary and Cheryl with me in addition to knowing the CWM Team plus other intercessors were praying back home. I was especially pleased because I knew God had called us to pray in this place. Located in Mitchells Plain the housing, education and employment was poor. Gangs ravaged and manipulated this community, killing anyone who stood in their way and taking young women as their sex slaves. We planned to go on their turf to pray, to pray on to the field where the fights start and where many had been killed. We knew they would be watching us, but it was time to take back this ground that had been in Satan's hands for too long.

More than sixty of us gathered, people of all ages from grandparents to babies in arms; whole families and from all backgrounds. Everyone had made a decision that it was time for change! We started with a short time of praise and worship, before I shared from Isaiah 61:1-4:

> *"The Spirit of the Sovereign Lord is on me, because the Lord has anointed me to proclaim good news to the poor. He has sent me to bind up the broken-hearted, to proclaim freedom for the captives and release from darkness for the prisoners, to proclaim the year of the Lord's favour and the day of vengeance of our God, to comfort all who mourn, and provide for those who grieve in Zion – to bestow on them a crown of beauty instead of ashes, the oil of joy instead of mourning, and a garment of praise instead of a spirit of despair. They will be called oaks of righteousness, a planting of the Lord for the display of his splendour. They will rebuild the ancient ruins and restore the places long devastated; they will renew the ruined cities that have been devastated for generations".*

I encouraged everyone that God had chosen, anointed and appointed them with authority to understand they were there for such a time as this. They were there to pray and to bring great breakthrough for their families and for their community.

I then shared from Jeremiah 1:5-10:

> *"'Before I formed you in the womb, I knew you, before you were born, I set you apart; I appointed you as a prophet to the nations.' 'Alas, Sovereign Lord,' I said, 'I do not know how to speak; I am too young.'*

> *But the Lord said to me, 'Do not say, "I am too young". You must go to everyone I send you to and say whatever I command you. Do not be afraid of them, for I am with you and will rescue you,' declares the Lord. Then the Lord reached out his hand and touched my mouth and said to me, 'I have put My words in your mouth. See, today I appoint you over nations and kingdoms to uproot and tear down, to destroy and overthrow, to build and to plant.'"*

Again, I encouraged these precious people that they could stand in the gap between history and destiny, by standing between heaven and earth to see God's kingdom come powerfully on earth. They could choose to be a mouthpiece to release God's word to uproot what the enemy had planted and to prophetically release God's peace and goodness.

Before we left the church, Cheryl began repenting powerfully on behalf of the white community for the historical abuse of the coloured communities. Pastor Jonathan received the repentance and released forgiveness on behalf of his community. He then spoke of the white people that had come to get the men drunk whilst their women and young people were taken as slaves. Gary responded, crying out in repentance and once again the people of JCC responded with lots of tears, releasing forgiveness to Cheryl and Gary as they represented the white people. This was such a powerful start to our prayer walk and we had not even left the building yet.

Next, we asked the Holy Spirit to reveal if there was anything wrong in our hearts before we took communion together. We kept some of the bread and the juice to take out with us and then we quietly walked over to the field, trying not to draw too much attention to ourselves.

Historically the field was the first place of bloodshed in Mitchell's Plain around 1986 and has been the site of regular bloodshed ever since. Mitchell's Plain was named after Major Charles Cornwallis Mitchell, a Freemason from Cornwall. Sadly, this was the site of much bloodshed on Wednesday evening, only a few minutes before we arrived at the church.

Now the field was barren of life, but full of empty beer bottles, broken glass and evidence of drug taking. It was dry and dusty as there had been no rain for many months and a season of drought had been declared. I could feel people's eyes watching us from every home surrounding the field and from every hiding place. Everyone was looking to me for guidance as we crossed over on to the field and my heart was thumping, but thankfully my eyes were fixed on God.

I heard the Lord whisper that I needed to model what we should do. So, we began our time on the field by me kneeling to repent on behalf of the British for releasing a dictatorial spirit and freemasonry into the land. It was a scary thing to do, the field was filthy, with all kinds of rubbish and I was an easy target for anyone if they wanted to take a shot at me. I went down on my knees, where I was prompted by the Lord to repent on behalf of Liverpool for our role in the transatlantic slave trade and the trauma affected upon Africa as a result of that. As I opened my eyes, Pastor Jonathan was beside me with those from JCC surrounding us on their knees too.

I asked for those who had been involved in gangs and crime or felt they had things to repent of on behalf of their community, to come into the centre and kneel if they could. We then surrounded them in a big circle to protect them from prying eyes, after all they would still be living there when we were back in Liverpool. We encouraged those who had come out of the gangs, to pray repentance on behalf of what they had done or what they had seen done. They did not need much encouragement as quickly the ex-gang members came to the middle and fell to their knees, weeping and crying from their hearts to God in real deep repentance. They began to repent for the murders and violence they had committed, for the women they had raped and the people they had seduced into the gangs.

One young man (I will call John) stood quietly and then looked at one of the young women (I will call Freda) at the edge of the crowd. Freda was a beautiful young teenage mum who looked very vulnerable, with a baby only a few months old. This was an incredible moment as John's big brown eyes filled with huge tears until they were flowing down his face. People all around began to weep and you could just hear people gently sobbing. The crowd began to shuffle about until there was a gap, leaving John facing a very sad-faced Freda, with barely a few yards between them. John took a big deep breath and in between sobs, he began to confess, repent and apologise to Freda for killing her brother! Freda looked broken and fragile as her knees buckled under her and she began to sob. I ran across to Freda and swept her into my arms, whilst she sobbed and sobbed. A little while later Freda turned to John with tears still flowing down her face and whispered that she forgave him. I am not so naïve to believe that all will be instantly well with them, but I know Pastor Jonathan will be there to help them process the truth and to bring healing to them. Many of us wept as the repentance and forgiveness was being poured out so powerfully.

Next a tall young man moved to the centre, with tears pouring down his face as he explained his past life of very serious drug addiction. He sobbed as he apologised for beating and robbing his mother who suddenly stepped forward and began to pray. Instead of simply forgiving her son, she too began to repent that she had treated him badly because she had been so angry with him and her heart had been full of bitterness towards God. They finished by forgiving one another and passionately hugging! Wow!

The next moment her husband stepped forward and joined them in the circle. He was not the son's real father and had been so angry with his stepson for the way he had robbed his precious wife. He repented of his anger towards this young man who had not come under his authority, resulting in him being thrown out of their home. He had watched him leave in horror as he disappeared and was swallowed up into the gangs. They then repented personally and on behalf of fathers and sons, ending again with lots of tears, forgiveness and big hugs. Reconciliation and healing come when we are prepared to humble ourselves and repent.

The floodgates of repentance were open as a young pretty woman repented of prostitution and drugs. Another woman, a mother of teenage sons stepped into the middle, falling upon her knees and beginning to cry out in repentance because she had hidden guns, ammunition, money and drugs thinking she was protecting her children. Next, two men stood facing one another in the middle and I held my breath, as I was a little afraid that they may have been about to start a fight. It turned out that in the past they had been members of opposing gangs and had done all they could to kill one another and yet somehow, they had both ended up in JCC. Clearly it was only God's plans for their lives that had enabled them both to survive their mutual attacks! Once again forgiveness flowed from one to the other and they were soon lovingly hugging one another, and you could tell that God had set them both free.

Another older woman stepped forward and shakily stooped down on to her knees. She cried out to God in great remorse. She had not only been a drug-dealer, but she had recruited many young people to deal drugs for her too. She confessed that she had sold drugs in most of the local schools and was responsible for many people becoming addicted to drugs. The deep repentance was so real and very powerful.

When everyone else had finished praying, Pastor Jonathan stepped into the middle and once again got down upon his knees in the midst of his congregation. He humbly began to repent on behalf of all of the church leaders, who had not been good spiritual fathers or led well across Mitchell's Plain.

Finally, the intercessors stepped forward and together we poured the remaining wine from our time of communion on to the ground to represent the cleansing blood of Jesus. Then Jonathan and I poured water on to the ground to complete the cleansing and to symbolise the release of the Holy Spirit. As we finished praying, a fine rain began to fall, as if to demonstrate a shift of atmospheres after months of drought.

We made our way back across to JCC giving thanks to Jesus for all He had done. However, God had not quite finished! We were about to celebrate with a fabulous feast the church had prepared for us all, when a distressed young man appeared. He was struggling with drugs himself but had been watching us all on the field and had simply followed us in to JCC. Within a few minutes he gave his life to Jesus and he had a huge smile on his face. We then proceeded to hungrily tuck into the delicious food and celebrate the huge breakthrough for everyone there and for the community.

ORPHAN HEARTS

We returned to JCC on Sunday where the feedback from the previous day was really amazing, everyone was buzzing about what God had done. We had a great morning and I shared about the orphan spirit and how we should be children of God. This is very important as until we deal with an orphan spirit, we are damaged, and we can cause so much pain to those around us. When we live as orphans we often stand in the way of the Holy Spirit and focus instead on finding our sense of value in our works instead of who we are in Christ. Paul declares:

> *"For you did not receive the spirit of slavery to fall back into fear, but you have received the Spirit of adoption as sons, by whom we cry, 'Abba! Father!'"* Romans 8:15 (ESV)

> *"For he chose us in him before the creation of the world to be holy and blameless in his sight. In love he predestined us for adoption to sonship through Jesus Christ, in accordance with his pleasure and will".* Ephesians 1:4-5

I found this simple tool very helpful to identify areas of my life where I needed healing from an orphan spirit.

Orphan Spirit	Child of God
Insecure	Secure
Critical and defensive	Loved and accepted
Jealous of others' success	Committed to others' success
Intimidated by others' success	Celebrates others' success
Serves to earn Father's love	Enjoys acceptance and favour
Feels alienated and lonely	Enjoys God's loving presence
Driven by need for approval	Led by the Spirit
Uses people to fulfill goals	Releases people to bless others
Repels spiritual children	Draws spiritual children
Struggles with rejection	You feel loved and you belong
Operates in anger and manipulates	Rests in the Father's love
Lacks trust	Trusts God
Always competes with others	Blesses others
Identity comes from being better than others	Identity comes as child of God; always wants to bless others
Lacks self-esteem	Walks in love and acceptance
You do not love yourself and struggle to love others.	Walks confidently in the love and joy of the Lord
Materialistic and concerned about appearances	Loves being God's child
Draws attention to yourself	Happy to be in the background
Violent and rebellious	Enjoys peace and understands authority

When we truly accept that we are adopted into God's family as son and daughters, the power of the orphan spirit is broken off our lives. There is immeasurably more available for each one of us as children; we can know our emotional identity, walk in our God-given destiny and embrace the eternal resources that God has for us. Sonship is so important that all creation is presently crying out for the manifestation of the mature sons of God (Romans 8:19)!

I shared how I had lived as an orphan for many years and how that had affected both my life and my family. (Read my story in *Extravagant Fire*.) I described the shift that came when I realised that God loved me, and I was His beloved empowered daughter. We had a great response as many people recognised that they had also been living as orphans. Boom!!! Now that was a massive breakthrough for so many!!

The following day, Ray Wilson had arranged for us to meet the Provisional Minister of Community Safety for the Western Cape, Dan Plato. We were joined by Jacqui Schmidt and it was great to hear Dan's heart and passion to see things positively change across the whole region. He was amazed to hear that we had already spent a week in Mitchell's Plain, witnessing for ourselves first-hand the impact of the gangs and the deaths in Eastridge. We shared our stories and spent some quality time praying for Dan before we left.

Cheryl worked as Chaplain at Robin's Trust which provides training and care for those who need nursing care, both before they go home from hospital and when they return home. On Tuesday it was our joy to visit and speak to two classes of student nurses from across Africa. Norma and I spoke, and the students sang! Wow, the sound was amazing!

During our visit, we ministered to William who thought nobody ever noticed him. He was thrilled to receive prayer and a card containing a prophetic word. We prayed and prophesied over most of the staff and those there to receive nursing. We gave them all a sealed envelope with a prophecy card containing a word of encouragement written by our CWM Team and people from Openwell Church in Southport. Clearly, we had no idea what was written inside each card and we simply trusted God that the right person would receive the card with a prophetic word especially written for them. It was a special time for us, and we heard that it had been a very precious time for all the people we encountered. Where the Spirit of the Lord is, there is freedom and healing! Thank you, Holy Spirit! Here are just some of the testimonies we received. I have changed their names for confidentiality purposes:

Amahle said, "Thank you so much. I had the most powerful revealing experience with God. The ladies prayed for me and gave me a card. I read it and it was definitely written for me personally. How could God know at that time, that I needed it? It was a revelation. It was an experience I have never ever had or felt so intensely. I needed God at that time. It was the right time, the right place, the right prayer. God is Great. It felt like God lifted the curtain and let the sunshine in on my life again."

Leah said, "They are women of strength. They encouraged me so deeply it was God-sent. I was not myself for the last two weeks and I was struggling to pray. They laid hands on me and I felt the anointing of the Holy Spirit and I was convicted that I needed to let go, and I did. I experienced breakthrough and I feel like a new person. Thank you so much."

We had a great morning followed by a wonderful afternoon, when we had the honour and joy of baptising Penny, who had wanted to be baptised for over twenty years. What a blessing for us to baptise our friend and then to celebrate afterwards with a great feast.

Prophecy fulfilled

Each time we have visited Cape Town we have been blessed to meet up with Steve Swart MP in Parliament. This time was extra special as Chuck Pierce and his team were also there. The meeting was packed tight with MPs, councillors, prophets, church leaders, intercessors and other guests. The Queen of Lopopo was there alongside representatives of the Khoi people and the Chief Justice of South Africa. It was good to catch up with Councillor Gerald, Pastor Daniel and many of our friends once again. We were shown to our reserved seats on the front row and warmly welcomed in Parliament by Steve Swart who greeted the VIPs. We were amazed to get a mention and even the little key we had given Steve last year got a mention too.

The Chief Justice brought a magnificent word from the Lord before Chuck Pierce gave his contribution finishing with a prophetic word for Cape Town and the nation. Next the Queen of Lopopo, the Chief Justice and a representative of the Khoi people made some powerful declarations over South Africa. The proceedings were soon finalised, and they invited everyone to join them to pray at 3pm at Signal Point.

After Parliament, we made our way to the Rhodes Memorial where there is a lovely restaurant and we could relish the amazing views over Cape Town. We had just finished our gorgeous lunch when we noticed protection vehicles arriving with the Chief Justice and all the entourage. We realised that the prayer meeting had been moved to the Rhodes Memorial! So, we were once again in the right place, at the right time with the right people to do what God wanted to be done.

It was good to join Ann Tate and the rest of Chuck's team as we all prayed and made declarations at the very site we had prayed at two years earlier. Finally, the Chief Justice prayed and anointed the ground to release new beginnings. What a great man of God he is and what a blessing for South Africa.

On Saturday we were thrilled to host a Big PUSH style meeting at New Life Vineyard Church in Pinelands. (Big PUSH is an incredible gathering of Christians from all church backgrounds that we host in Liverpool. There is amazing praise and worship, lots of prayer, prophecy and preaching). We were especially pleased to be joined by some of the intercessors from Eastridge in Mitchell's Plain plus Mama Thandi and the Annas from the townships of Khayelitsha and Gugulethu. With their arrival we had great representation from the black, white and coloured communities. This is highly unusual as these precious communities do not usually mix together. We had a great time of worship and some powerful times of prayer.

We prayed for the Annas first, beautiful black ladies with the most gorgeous faces full of character and love for Jesus. What a joy for us to bless and honour them. Then we prayed for those from Eastridge, honouring them for all that happened last Saturday at the Prayer Walk. People were deeply moved as we shared the story of how so many people had poured out prayers of repentance and forgiveness on that field of blood.

We enjoyed singing together and those who could came out to join in the dancing. You could see the strongholds breaking as Jesus built bridges with his deep love and compassion. We prayed for the mothers and fathers, as God desires to restore families, and fathers in particular as in Malachi 4:6 *"He will turn the hearts of the fathers to the children, and the hearts of the children to their fathers, lest I come and strike the earth with a curse".* We prayed for Jacqui, Thandi and Jasmine representing three mothers, from the three communities, who together have the potential to mobilise many people to pray across Cape Town.

Finally, we prayed for each group, starting with the white people. Jasmine and her coloured ladies quickly came to pray but the Annas needed more encouragement. What we had not realised was that these precious ladies had experienced many years of life as the servants of the white people, so it was a huge leap for them to come out to lay hands on them and pray. However, they did eventually come, and it was another very profound and powerful time of breakthrough.

During our final day of this trip we travelled to Stellenbosch with Jacqui and Carl, where we ministered in the Vineyard Church. I prayed and prophesied with Hans. God told me he had a very powerful testimony and he needed to share it, as God was going to use it to touch many lives. Prophetically, I saw him holding huge bolt cutters and felt the Lord was going to use him to bring freedom and deliverance to many. Hans' mouth was open wide and eventually he began to tell me that in November 2015, he was diagnosed with a severe brain aneurism. Sadly, the doctors had given up hope of him having a full recovery, expecting him to be brain damaged. However, God had saved him against all the odds! Hans then went on to tell us that he had been training for deliverance ministry. So, he was very encouraged and so was I! Thank you, Jesus!

We went for lunch and spent some time praying and prophesying over our waitress. She was a lovely joy-filled Christian who was studying and looking after her young family. She was thrilled and blessed, and again so were we. We prayed about what to give her as a tip and gave well over the usual amount to bless her. She wept as we gave her the tip and explained that she had been crying out to God as she was desperately short financially.

Pastor Daniel (from Parliament) came to visit us as we were finishing off our final packing. I had a word of knowledge for him and I was pleased to hear that it was accurate. We had a lovely time catching up with what God had been doing in his life and how things were developing in Parliament. We were glad to have time to pray for him once again.

Then we were off to fulfil our last appointment at New Life Church. During the worship we sang "How Great Is Our God" and I was in floods of tears at just how great God had been during this trip. We had a tremendous evening and I shared some of the stories of what God had done during our time in Cape Town, including the repentance in the field, the time in Parliament and the Big PUSH. I also shared how God is looking to see people empowered and fulfilling their destinies. At the end of the evening so many people came up to greet us and to tell us that their hope had been restored. We were really blessed when Pastor John came with a couple of others to pray for us.

All that was left for us was to say our goodbyes to everyone and thank God once again, for one of our greatest adventures YET!

PRAYER: Thank you for the destiny upon my life. Heavenly Father I pray that you will fill me with your Holy Spirit and release your favour upon my life so that I may live to bring you glory. Amen.

Facing Your Fears

South Africa March 2017

For me, this next trip was one of my most challenging on many levels and particularly because our team was dramatically reduced at the last minute. There should have been four of us, Norma and I flying out first and then my husband Steve and our friend Chris Higgins flying out for the second week. Chris was so excited about his first trip to South Africa, however very sadly he went to be with Jesus just five weeks before our departure. That was so painful and hard! Then, just a few days prior to our departure, Norma had to drop out due to a very painful back injury.

I must admit I had a little wobble at the prospect of travelling alone, as I had never done that before. I used to be so fearful of travelling anywhere, however thankfully Jesus had set me free. Despite that, I was far more comfortable with the prospect of travelling with a team. I always love to follow what Jesus modelled as He sent people out in teams of at least two people and if that was good enough for Jesus that was good enough for me. However, as I spoke to my husband Steve, he encouraged me to go as he was going to fly out to join me half-way through the trip. If I was still in any doubt about going, the Lord had been speaking to me about Jonah for months. Jonah had ended up in the belly of a whale because he refused to go where God had called him to go!

God had told me many years ago, that He would never leave or forsake me. Over the years He never has, and that was the reality for me as I travelled: I knew my heavenly Father was with me. The importance of being in the right place, with the right people, at the right time and doing the right thing was so important for this trip.

Despite being personally more than a little challenged, I landed at Cape Town Airport early Friday evening and it was a joy to be collected by our friends Carl and Jacqui. I enjoyed their company as we had a meal together before I was dropped off at my hotel for the night. However, there was no lift and as I was struggling with my luggage on the stairs, I stumbled. I put my hands out to save myself and really injured my right hand. I am right-handed! I was exhausted by the time I got to my room but decided that tomorrow was another day, with an early start, and that my hand would be ok.

Saturday, I woke at 5am and quickly showered, but really struggled to dry my hair with my gammy hand. I had an early flight to Durban to meet our friend Dias Isaacs and then together we had more travelling ahead. It was a scenic flight, flying over the beautiful South African countryside, with undulating mountains, lakes and colourful coastlines.

At this point, if I had any doubts that I was doing the right thing, in the right place, at the right time, meeting the right people, to do the right thing, they disappeared as I walked through Durban Airport. There was an amazing art sculpture of a giant whale on the wall! God gave me a huge sign to confirm He was with me, despite my painful hand.

I was thrilled to spend time with Dias again and, after a five-hour drive, we arrived at our destination QwaQwa in the Free State! We were warmly welcomed by Dias's precious Indian friends, Jaya and Ekbal (names have been changed). They not only owned the local clothing factories, but also lead the local church in a converted factory unit, now complete with a platform and crystal chandeliers!

FACTORY CHURCH

It was a delight to spend time with Jaya and Ekbal and to hear what God had laid on their hearts for their local community. The next morning, we enjoyed church with a congregation made up with lots of children and young people, plus many families. This particular Sunday there were a lot of visitors too and a great sense of excitement. Dias shared and then I spoke on the story of (you guessed it) Jonah! We had a powerful time as God's presence was so strong and we were thrilled to see over twenty people give their lives to Jesus. Lives were changed by the word of God and His presence! Praise God!

Early Monday morning we toured their four factories: we watched the huge rolls of fabrics arriving, the fabric being cut, the garments being stitched together and the packaging. How often we get dressed and never give a thought to the designers, the pattern makers, the cutters, the machinists, the packers and all those people involved in making our clothing! I was reminded of my mum-in-law who had spent many years bent over a sewing machine working in a clothing factory.

It was an awesome privilege to visit these busy factory floors and to share the Gospel with so many people. Then Ekbal told them what God had done in his life over the weekend, describing how he had been living his life as Jonah – running away from God. I was thankful for his humble heart and obedience in turning back to God. After he shared, the presence of God came powerfully as we prayed for over a thousand precious people across the factory floor.

It took us most of the day to travel back to Durban before I flew back to Cape Town. I received a lovely message, *"I want to say thank you for your obedience, love and support. You were truly God sent as Ekbal said, "Many people have come our way, but through you, God had impacted him the most. Well God has sent the 'Elijah' to 'Jonah' – thank you."*

Wow! I hit the road running in Cape Town! First thing on Tuesday I met with the Ministers Fraternal of Gugulethu; a very violent and poor black township. Sadly, in this community people were being murdered and/or raped most days. You really need to know your way in and your way out, as you cannot risk getting lost here! I was very grateful to Mario and Latasha for taking me and for "Mama Thandi" for carefully guiding us in. The leaders were so hungry for more of God and gave me the biggest welcome, as they were desperate to see breakthrough come in their community. Our friend Thandi introduced me as her spiritual mother, which was a great honour for me, as she is so loved by her communities.

Breakthrough with dead bodies

Thandi's testimony was truly incredible and so encouraging to us. We invest all that God wants us to, in one person's life at a time, and often never get to hear what happened to them or through them after that. You may recall we first met her briefly at Engedi Church during our visit in 2015. Thandi told us her story, she described how she had not agreed with people falling on the floor and was determined that would never happen to her. However, towards the end of the evening we gave her one of our prophetic keys to open up doors of the kingdom and we laid hands on her: moments later the Lord came upon her in power and she was down on the floor, complete with her high heels! Thandi could not move for over half an hour as God was massively at work in her life depositing a fresh impartation of his love, power and authority. Thandi has never regretted those moments on the floor because they changed her life and we know that through her, God has changed the lives of many more people too.

You may recall, early during our 2016 trip, Ray Wilson had invited us to speak at a meeting attended by many bishops, church leaders and General Brandt (the police chief of Khayelitsha). Afterwards, I had introduced General Brandt to Thandi and challenged them both to work together to solve two difficult cases. General Brandt asked Thandi for prayer about two desperate situations with incredible "God" results:

1) A girl was gang raped, murdered and her body left in a public toilet in Khayelitsha. The police had two suspects but insufficient evidence so Thandi and her team of intercessors began to pray. It was not long before a witness was found, who was able to give unshakable evidence in court leading to the conviction of all the suspects.

2) Anelisa Dulaze was snatched on the eve of her 21st birthday and killed. The police did not know who had done this or where her body was. Meanwhile one of the intercessors, who was part of Thandi's Annas Prayer group, had been concerned about her son for some time and asked for prayer. A few days later there was a knock on Thandi's door, and this young man was standing there. He told her he was carrying a heavy burden and then began to confess that he had sex with Anelisa, before they had fought, and she had "accidentally died". Panic-stricken he had buried her body!

Thandi called General Brandt who sent Officers to arrest the young man. He confessed, was imprisoned, and was awaiting sentencing whilst we were there. Then Thandi had the terrible job of taking General Brandt to uncover Anelisa's body. A short while later she was assisting with the heartbreaking task of telling Anelisa's mother that they had found her precious daughter's body.

Thandi asked the Lord to use her as a peacemaker and to help to bring justice for both these broken-hearted mothers. The whole community was ready to turn violently against the intercessor and her family, but the Lord used Thandi very powerfully to bring peace in the community and between these two devastated families.

Hearing of all this, a woman asked Thandi to pray as she needed help. Her nephew was Khangayi Sedumedi known as the “Century City serial killer”. He worked as a security guard in the suburb of Century City Shopping Centre and had connected with girls over Facebook, offering them jobs. As six women responded to his offer of employment, he met them individually to take them to their non-existent jobs; instead, he raped, killed, and then buried them. He was now in prison serving six life sentences, but the problem was his own mother had been missing for some time. This precious woman’s sister was missing, and she knew in her heart that her nephew was responsible. However, he would not admit it or tell them where her body was. This woman was desperate to get some closure and to lay her sister to rest. She asked Thandi and the Annas to pray.

A few days after they had prayed, Khangayi confessed to the prison governor what he had done and where his mother’s body could be found. At last the family were able to bury this poor mother’s body with dignity.

And there was more! Ray Wilson was very encouraged as he told us that the police medal parade had been held on 5th May 2016. Publicly, General Brandt had thanked the intercessors for their sterling work, which he said, “Proves that God hears and answers our prayers”. The Deputy Commissioner remarked afterwards, “He recognised that this was the move of the Holy Spirit”. Sadly, a day after hearing this amazing news from Ray, I heard that Ray had gone to be with Jesus.

Back to 2017 and our meeting with the Ministers Fraternal of Gugulethu. I spoke for 45 minutes and then prayed for all the leaders. However, despite going over time, they asked me to continue, so we had a question and answer session. This brought them more revelation and all they could keep saying was Wow! Wow! Wow! They begged me to come back the following week despite it being a national bank holiday. There was such a sense that God could move here very powerfully as they were really desperate for change!

The following evening, I was pleased to return to JCC in Eastridge led by our friend Pastor Jonathan Naicker. It was wonderful to see so many of our friends once again and to witness people coming to Christ.

Thursday morning, we had breakfast with Alfie Fabe who is the spiritual Papa to so many across the area and the nations. Alfie has raised up and empowered so many sons and daughters. He is an incredible real role model to me, as I long to be a good spiritual mum myself to many across the nations.

I was pleased to have the opportunity to speak to the "non-church" group at JCC later that morning. I loved it, as many drug addicts, alcoholics and broken people came, who would never go inside a church. It was wonderful to share Jesus' love with almost 80 people. I spoke, shared my testimony and the Holy Spirit riveted people to their seats, with many people in tears. At the end of the morning many people gave their lives to Jesus. One precious Muslim woman asked me to pray for her and her friend who had been sexually abused since she was four years old.

Friday morning was very precious and refreshing, as I spent time with Nathan and Janine Asher in Stellenbosch. They have been leading the Victory Outreach Church and rehabilitation house for drug addicts and alcoholics in Mitchell's Plain for three years. Wherever you go, God has his people serving and reaching out – what a blessing!

Saturday was the day I had been waiting for as Steve arrived – yeah!!!! I had a nice surprise and divine appointment at the airport, as I bumped into Pastor Daniel who now ministers in Parliament. It was good to catch up on his encouraging news.

Sunday morning, I was at Tell Them Ministries Church led by Pastor Peter-John. Glory to God, Jesus healed two backs plus other healings, but the greatest miracle was five people giving their lives to Jesus and others returning to God.

After we finished there, we were collected to have lunch with Pastor Jonathan. It was a real joy to be back at JCC for the evening service where we had a great response from everyone. We finished with a powerful ministry time, praying for all the children and young people and once again people responded to the Gospel message. Thank you, God!

Ministering to leaders

On Monday, God moved powerfully as I spoke at the KMI leaders meeting. I am not sure if they were expecting a sweet message, but I really challenged them from the story of Elijah found in 1 Kings 17. Elijah brought a word from God declaring a drought upon the nation; he fled, leaving Jezebel and Ahab who then killed most of the prophets. There was not only a drought of water but also more seriously a drought of God's word! Here we were in Cape Town, a place currently in serious water drought and with very little accurate prophetic revelation of God's word.

Elijah fled to the Kerith Ravine where he made a covenant with God before he travelled to Zarephath the "place of the furnace". As he arrived at the Town Gates of Zarephath, he discovered a widow woman and her son who were preparing to die. Hopelessness, despair, and death were in the gates of Zarephath and I asked the leaders if they understood what was located in the gates of their community?

I knew what was in their gates, because I had just read a report written by Ricardo Mackenzie, a Member of the Western Cape Provincial Parliament. Ricardo stated there had been 119 murders, 179 sexual offences and 546 cases of assault reported in 2016. I had no doubt those numbers were only the tip of the iceberg, as most people do not even report offences or assaults, therefore it is very difficult for the police to keep an accurate track of the number of people missing or dead.

"It is time for the Church to arise, to declare a stop in the heavenly realms and a turning of this tide of evil". This was a prophetic word the Lord gave me in 2003 in Liverpool! It is time for the church everywhere to take responsibility for what is allowed in and out of the gates of their communities. After all, murders, sexual offences and assaults are certainly not part of God's plan for our communities!

Elijah's story continues, as he brought a sacrifice and called upon God for the fire – Cape Town and South Africa have dozens of prophetic words about the fire of God coming. However, I know God is calling the church to repentance, to restore the gates and to bring God's healing love and power to their communities. God is looking for an altar of prayer to be built by his whole church so He can send His revival fire!

Pastor Chris Sloster said, *"We pray that The Lord will continue to enlarge the territory of Sue's 'Kingdom mandate' and use her in unprecedented ways in these days. Humbled and honoured to be in covenant relationship with you Sue and Steve".*

Despite the thunder and lightning, plus a little rain on Monday evening, Tuesday was hotter than ever. At 98°F it was very, very hot and humid! I think God has a sense of humour, as I was speaking about the story of Elijah and the fiery furnace at the Ministers Fraternal in Gugulethu. I am sure we were experiencing furnace temperatures!

We were very hot when we arrived, so our hosts welcomed us with a glass of water. Overseas I would never normally drink a glass of water, but I did not have any bottled water and I was desperately thirsty. After a short time of worship, I was asked to speak. I shared the word the Lord had laid on my heart and we had a brilliant response again. I was blessed that Bishop Robert bought all my books and distributed them amongst the leaders! We finished at 12:30pm and drove straight to Heideveld (a coloured community) where we had a meeting hosted by Pastor William, with Thandi, the intercessors and more leaders. Wow, I love what God is doing here!

This too was a powerful time as Jacqui was waiting for us with lots of our white friends from Vineyard Church including John the pastor. They had kindly brought a delicious lunch for everyone and there was a great turn out from across the Churches. I mention this because the bridging of communities happens so rarely and when it does God certainly smiles. I spoke on Isaiah 61 and there was a great response. I challenged everyone about the importance of having accurate prophetic revelation for the leaders and the intercessors to work effectively with. There was a time of powerful repentance and forgiveness between the prophets, leaders and intercessors. I was thrilled that Pastor William invited Jacqui to return in the future, to teach on the prophetic in order to see a healthy prophetic ministry begin to emerge.

Do you really want me to go Lord?

Wednesday afternoon we planned to go to Steenberg Police Station in Lavender Hill with Jacqui and her friend Greg Kruyer. Lavender Hill was notorious for being a very violent area. Greg had been working with the police for a few weeks and encouraging people in the area to pray.

However, a very dangerous taxi war had started leaving the local people terrified. Taxi drivers were being attacked, shot, and sometimes killed by people from competing businesses. It was constantly on the news and everyone was talking about it. In the middle of this God wanted us to go into the police station in the heart of this community! We asked God, "Are you sure you really want us to go?", "Yes I do," God replied, almost surprised that we had even asked.

On top of that a beautiful thirteen-year-old child called Rene Roman (her name means "Reborn or Born Again") had been missing in the community for twelve days. The community had been earnestly searching for her and appealing for help. Sadly, the day before we were due to go, we heard that the police had discovered Rene's body in a shed. Horrifically, this precious child was found half-naked, bound hands and feet, rolled up in a carpet. She had been raped and murdered. We knew that this was going to make this really dangerous community even more volatile.

Even the staff at Howard's End where we were staying, were urging us not to go. So, I asked God again, "Are you really sure you want us to go?", "Yes, I do!" It is really important to know where God wants you to be – so you are always in the right place, at the right time, with the right people doing the right thing, so God can release heaven to earth. If you are not listening to God, you can find yourself in some very dangerous situations without bringing any breakthroughs.

We awoke nervously on Wednesday morning to the news that the police had arrested Andrew Plaatjies, one of the Roman family's neighbours. He had been taken into Steenberg Police Station, the very police station we were going to, in the middle of this very dangerous community. We did not know if we would be driving into a riot, as the local community responded to this devastating and shocking news. We threw up one last prayer, "God are you really sure you want us to go?" Again, we heard the Lord, "Yes I want you to GO!" It is at times like this that I am always very grateful that we have the CWM Team back home praying for us.

As Jacqui drove us into Lavender Hill, we were very thankful that all looked quiet and calm. Jacqui managed to park right outside Steenberg Police Station, which was a big answer to prayer. We nervously stepped out of the car, not knowing what to expect but recognising that God was pleased that we had chosen to be obedient and not give in to our fears.

Despite the terrible circumstances, we were pleased to have an incredibly significant meeting with Colonel Alexander, Greg Kruyer and their team of intercessors. This little team included one precious woman who lived in the same neighbourhood as Rene Roman's family. Amazingly her name was also Rene! The meeting was exceptional, as we prayed and anointed them all with oil and released a prophetic word to Colonel Alexander and to Greg. We spent some time praying for Rene Roman's family, the community, and the police.

It was good to meet Greg afterwards and to connect with his heart for the whole of Africa. He shared some incredible stories of his times with the traditional Kings and Queens of South Africa as God was using him to bring powerful cleansing, healing and reconciliation.

Colonel Alexander messaged me later and said, *"Thanks for the encouragement, prayers, the blessings, as well as the revelation by the Holy Spirit, it was awesome to be in the presence of the Lord!"* We gave thanks to God for His protection and all that He did.

ARMED POLICE ESCORT

Thursday was another amazing day! The importance of being in the right place, with the right people, at the right time and doing the right thing was so important on this day in particular. Our friend Thandi invited us to pray with her and the police in the gates of Khayelitsha. We really had to pray as mass violence had broken out across many of the communities after Rene's body was discovered a couple of days earlier. The on-going taxi war between the gangs was also spreading, with vans being burnt out and people being shot across many of the townships. Even many of the local people were terrified!

In the midst of this we went to the township of Khayelitsha, where people live in the most appalling conditions! There are thousands of tiny little tin shacks packed so tightly together, in some of the worst living conditions you can imagine. Besides the roads that go through the very centre of the township and around the exterior, there are no other access roads. Hence it has become a bedrock of violence, crime and depravity. It is too dangerous for even the police and emergency services to enter most of these communities.

This community was so dangerous, that the police insisted on meeting us on the motorway to escort us into the police station. As they carefully led us through the packed streets, we were very grateful, as we knew we would never have found the way ourselves. Goodness knows where we would have ended up or what may have happened to us!

We met in General Brandt's huge office although sadly he was not available after some surgery, but his Deputy was hosting us in his absence. The room was filled with pastors, leaders and intercessors whom Thandi had managed to assemble. We enjoyed an amazing time of worship, before I shared some of our story and we had a powerful time of prayer together. It would have been very difficult for us to drive around Khayelitsha by convoy and not get lost in the midst of this sprawling and dangerous township. So, we were grateful that the police had supplied one of their armoured buses to transport the intercessors, church leaders and police officers around together. We felt very special and safe as we also had armed police vehicles at the front and rear of our bus escorting us.

Our first stop was the fire station – this is the place where at least five or six dead bodies are deposited by the gangs every weekend: that's a lot of sons, daughters, fathers, brothers and friends! They are forced to deal with horrific situations almost every day. The fire officers were deeply touched by God's love, with many in floods of tears as we prayed for them and thanked them for all they do.

Our next stop was a shopping complex which marked the gateway into Khayelitsha. The police said this was a particularly dangerous area, however we chose not to be intimidated. Instead we had a powerful time of worship, repentance and prayer, declaring the Lordship of Jesus over that community. This finished with a real outbreak of joy with everyone hugging the police; and they loved it! They had never been encouraged before and were really overwhelmed.

Once again, we all climbed back into our armoured "Prayer" bus and drove to the area where the Indian bride Anni Dewani was killed on 13th November 2010. She and her husband were on their honeymoon in Cape Town when their taxi was allegedly hijacked as they drove through Khayelitsha. Everyone believed her husband Shrien was involved with Anni's murder yet, despite him being taken to court, it was found that crucial evidence was missing, so the case against him was dismissed. We took some time to pray for justice.

TRANSFER OF POWER

As we were driving around Khayelitsha we heard from Greg and Colonel Alexander that trouble was brewing in Lavender Hill. The police had taken the murderer to the location where Rene's body had been found and a huge crowd had assembled and were attacking the police. One officer had sustained serious injuries, vehicles were being destroyed, shots were being fired and many fires were being started.

We immediately stopped to pray, and later we were pleased to hear from Greg Kruyer about Rene Smith (who works in the community). Rene ran immediately to see Rene Roman's mother (the murdered child) and appealed to her to tell the community to stop the violence. This precious mother stood in front of the violent mob, demanding that they cease the violence, as that would not bring her beloved daughter back. Amazingly, as she did, peace was restored. Rene Smith called for the community to bring their children out so they could dedicate them to God and pray for their protection. Suddenly the whole situation turned around and this rioting community, began to pray. Now that is extravagant breakthrough!

Greg said, *"You are here to witness the transfer of power. It's the birthing pains of transformation. Glad you could be here to witness it and agree with us for complete victory".*

Rene Smith said, *"Last week after we met and you prayed for me, I felt a shift in my spirit. What an awesome impartation that I could take back to the local intercessors and community. Together we stand; divided we fall. Revival, acceleration and Godly intervention in the affairs of man.*

Thank you, Sue for being a vessel of honour and for spreading the Father's love. What I received from you no ordinary man could impart. You brought new wine and new oil to these shores of Cape Town. Be blessed and keep the oil flowing into vessels of honour for His Glory.

I took that anointing and I imparted it to the prayer group the very next morning. They all fell under the anointing. I can't stop praising God for in the midst of the storm He is revealing and releasing His power. Prayers are reshaping our nation! Everything is coming together. The reporter asked if we can duplicate what is happening here in other areas too. God is faithful. Revival is here".

We drove around Khayelitsha for three hours praying and at the end of our time together we released the presence of God into the area. There was such a sense of breakthrough coming. We were grateful to the police again as they escorted us out of the area to the motorway safely.

We have much to thank God for, as we experienced so many breakthroughs . . . Glory to God! He was doing amazing things in our midst despite me having a bad tummy!

THE TWO TREES

The following day we made it into Parliament for our meeting with Steve Swart MP and his gorgeous wife Louise. We had an excellent time prophesying and praying for Steve and the government. I shared a picture I had a few days earlier:

I saw two trees: One was an ancient tree with no leaves, but the branches had snakes coiled on them and vultures perched on the top. The second tree was a young tree, beautiful and full of healthy life. The tree was still in a pot waiting to be transplanted in a good position.

I sensed the Lord was saying the first tree, the ancient tree, represented the government in South Africa. It was deeply rooted but was not bringing life. You could not move it by cursing it or praying against it. If you tried you would be attacked by the snakes and then finished off by the vultures. I could see as God's people prayed and declared truth, peace, righteousness and integrity etc.; it was as though they had spades and they were removing the earth from around the roots that had kept the tree stable.

God was calling His people to pray for those He had been preparing. When the earth around the evil roots was removed, suddenly a powerful wind came and wrapped around the tree, uprooting it and casting it aside. It was now time for the young sapling to be transplanted into position.

I felt the story of Mordecai was very significant for Steve Swart and that as he stood in the gates of the government of the nation, God would use him to expose the plans of the enemy. Interesting to note that Mordecai eventually became the second most powerful man in the nation.

Steve was keen to hear about all we had been up to across Cape Town during our time, and it was good to be able to bring some of the issues we had seen to him. Steve is a real minister for justice too . . . there is a pattern evolving here!

Steve Swart said, *"Thanks again for your faithfulness in praying for us in Parliament and for ministering in various Cape areas. It was great to host you and Steve at Parliament. God bless".*

Louise Swart said, *"What an incredible time together! WHAT A BLESSING! Thank you! GOD IS ON THE MOVE!"*

On Saturday morning, we gathered many people from across the different communities of Cape Town for a momentous occasion. It was not just that Thandi's testimony was incredible, but a black woman had never spoken in a mainly white church like this before. God was moving very powerfully through the teaching, the ministry times and in so many ways! Everyone was encouraged by the real local stories of what God was doing in their communities.

My tummy was still not right, and I had not managed to eat anything for a few days. Thankfully, up to now nobody had noticed as I was able to do everything I was required to do. However, Saturday afternoon, Steve and I decided to visit the beautiful waterfront in Cape Town, where there is a lovely mix of shops, bars and restaurants. I realised that I was feeling very weak, so we decided to break my fast and chose a lovely restaurant on the water's edge. Unfortunately, I was poorly again and so I visited a chemist who sold me some Imodium Melts which were supposed to work quickly. As soon as I took the medication, I had an allergic reaction and my head felt like it had suddenly been immersed under water. By the evening, my throat started to misbehave and my voice disappeared to no more than a whisper.

Thankfully, it was not painful, but I still had to preach at the Sunday morning service at New Life Church. However, I was stubbornly determined that despite having no more than a whisper for a voice, if they could pick up my voice on the microphone I would preach. Thanks to a wonderful sound guy, we managed to amplify my tiny whisper sufficiently for people to hear the message. It was good to see so many people sitting on the edges of their seats to listen to every word and I was encouraged by the massive response.

Praise God, it was amazing that I did not have to miss one speaking engagement. Throughout the days ahead my voice was no more than a croaky whisper, and it was funny that everyone felt they had to respond to me by whispering back again! All that remains for me is to stand in awe of God and to give Him all the glory for all that He did!

Later in the year we received an encouraging report of a seven thousand seat marquee being erected in the Lavender Hill area. Many hundreds of people encountered Jesus' love every day and we were thrilled to hear that some of the worst gang leaders gave their lives to Jesus. We then heard from Station Commander Jannie Alexander of Lavender Hill:

"Gang murders on average one per day in the Steenberg Precinct which includes the known hotspot of Lavender Hill. Figure dropped to 2 for the whole of following month and been low all along until August where we are happy to announce not a single murder in the precinct.

We give God all the glory for nothing is impossible with Him. Thank you to Sue from Liverpool who also prayed here with us. The local pastors for your support on the ground, the NGOs (Non-Governmental Organisations) for your hard work and dedication. This is a big one to celebrate. Hats off to you all. I'll say it again – not a single murder in Steenberg and Lavender Hill for the whole month of August".

A few months later Colonel Jannie Alexander was awarded a commendation and promoted, just as we had prophesied.

PRAYER: Thank you Lord that you give us all authority to pray and to see our communities shift. Please help us to take hold of that and to use it effectively to bring you glory. Amen.

MINISTERS OF JUSTICE

God calls us all to be Ministers of Justice and to move in His authority and power. As God's beloved children it is so important that we understand the authority we have because Jesus chose to die on the cross. Everything changed at the cross, absolutely everything! Justice is judgement that leads to a verdict of innocence or guilt with a suitable punishment. The world's justice system requires victims and offenders. However, because of Jesus, and the grace He releases, we do not have to be victims or offenders.

Matthew 12:18 quotes Isaiah 42 speaking about Jesus: *"Here is my servant whom I have chosen, the one I love, in whom I delight; I will put my Spirit on him, and he will proclaim justice to the nations"*. Jesus, full of God's Spirit, was destined to proclaim justice to the nations!! So, when we are full of the Holy Spirit, we too should be proclaiming justice in our families, communities and nations.

Matthew 12:20 quotes Isaiah 42:3: *"A bruised reed he will not break, and a smouldering wick he will not snuff out, till he has brought justice through to victory"*. This does not mean revenge! Justice is there for us all, but we need to claim it and intercede until we have brought it through to victory. However, too often we turn a blind eye to injustice unless it affects us.

The trouble is that when we turn a blind eye, we end up blind and hard-hearted! A good example of that was the Fetish slave girl we spotted walking on the road in Ghana. Slavery is against the law in Ghana and yet because Fetish temples go way back in the cultural history of Ghana, people do not consider that these slave girls and their captors are breaking the law even today.

Another example is the Hillsborough disaster which was the worst football disaster in the history of European football when 96 Liverpool fans died. Immediately, the cover up by the police, media and politicians began. The inquest verdicts of "accidental death" were an appalling injustice. The Hillsborough families appealed to the highest courts in the land, even as high as the European Court of Human Rights, and were consistently rejected.

However, they never gave up seeking the truth and neither did we! God told us that when the death shroud is lifted off Liverpool, revival will come! God led us to bring the breakthrough through by going into the courts of heaven where the scales of justice are always tipped in our favour as we pray. God gave us the strategy to stand in the gap and to intercede to bring heaven into this situation. We called on God and prophesied to disclose the truth and to bring justice until it came to earth!

In June 2005 we visited the Hillsborough Stadium for the first time to pray through the Justice Taylor report releasing forgiveness to all concerned. Then on 7th July 2009 we revisited the Hillsborough Stadium with a larger national prayer team. A short while later, in December 2009, the government set up the Hillsborough Independent Panel to review documents relating to the disaster. In September 2012, the panel produced a shocking report based on 450,000 pages of documents previously stored by the government, other public bodies, private companies, and individuals, supporting all that the families and survivors had declared.

A month later, the Attorney General applied for the original inquests to be quashed. In December 2012, following a campaign by the bereaved families, the High Court ordered a fresh hearing. The Hillsborough Inquest began on 31 March 2014 at a purpose-built courtroom in Warrington, Cheshire.

We visited the inquest on 11th March 2015 to pray – the second day of David Duckenfield giving evidence and the day that he turned to the families, admitted he had lied and then apologised. What a shift and breakthrough!

Why did that shift, and breakthrough come? David Duckenfield was giving evidence and there was a sense that he was not answering the questions that really mattered. People were becoming very frustrated in the court. So, I sat and prayed in the court until the Lord spoke to me very clearly, "Take a card out of your bag and write these words inside.

"Dear David,
We have been praying for you for many years. God wants us to tell you that He loves you very much and He wants to give you peace. Abundant blessings, Sue Sinclair"

I passed the card to the Court Clerk and asked her to pass it to David Duckenfield. After lunch, the whole atmosphere in the Court Room changed and David Duckenfield confessed and spoke of his sorrow! This was one of the breakthroughs we had been waiting to hear for decades. Many of us were in floods of tears!

On Tuesday 26th April 2016 the jury returned their verdict:

- 96 fans were unlawfully killed
- The fans were not responsible
- The stadium had structural defects
- The emergency services contributed to the loss of life.

The death shroud is lifting off Liverpool! Since then we have seen God moving increasingly across Liverpool. We really believe that revival is on the way!

In our nations, the Ministry of Justice is part of the function of our governments. In the Kingdom of Heaven, there is a ministry of justice that falls upon the shoulders of the Church to take hold of and apply. In Micah 6:8 (ESV) God tells us, what is good; and what He requires of us – *"to do justice, and to love kindness, and to walk humbly with our God."*

Theodore Roosevelt said, "Justice consists not in being neutral between right and wrong, but in finding out the right and upholding it, wherever found, against the wrong"[4].

Haile Selassie said, "Throughout history, it has been the inaction of those who could have acted, the indifference of those who should have known better, the silence of the voice of justice when it mattered most, that has made it possible for evil to triumph"[5].

Our role as God's children is to stand in the gap for justice for our lives, for our families, for our communities and nations.

PRAYER: Heavenly Father I thank you for Jesus, that he was full of God's Spirit and was destined to proclaim justice to the nations! So, I ask that you continue to fill your people with Holy Spirit, so that we too will be proclaimers of justice in our families, communities and nations.

---

4. Theodore Roosevelt, *Fear God and Take Your Own Part* (New York: George H. Doran, 1916)
5. Emperor Selassie's speech on inaction cited as from an address in Addis Ababa (1963)

Breakthrough At The President's Back Door

Pam Shaw and I arrived in Washington DC in September 2015 on our way to minister at a conference in Franklin, Virginia. We were welcomed by Marvin and immediately knew we had our first divine appointment as he poured his heart out to us. When all of the other conference speakers had arrived from Rwanda, South Africa, Kenya, Nigeria, Liberia, and areas of USA, we travelled together to our hotel in Franklin, Virginia. We were thankful for the large comfortable bus as we drove through the storm-filled streets.

There were many opportunities for us to pray for people in our hotel. When we noticed people arriving for the church that met there, Pam and I slipped in and asked if we could pray to bless them. They were really surprised by these two white women and encouraged as we prayed for them.

Three churches had joined together to host us, and their generosity was staggering. Our host churches had gathered together, with all their congregations and we were given the biggest welcome ever! The powerful worship was off the scale and the four preachers one after the other, all brought anointed messages.

This is a black community and many of these beautiful people would have been around when Dr Martin Luther King was leading the way in the battle for equality. This was so humbling for Pam and me, as the only two little white faces in their midst.

The days were a great mix of excellent teaching and interaction with the local community. It was fantastic to visit Franklin High School, where we were given a tour and the opportunity to pray for the headteacher, staff and children.

The evening celebrations were powerful and we witnessed Jesus pouring out His love. The church was full, with more church leaders attending than had ever come together before. Apostle Peggy Scott spoke from her heart and said, "I believe there is a spiritual awakening here in Franklin". After the teaching came the fire!!! There was a powerful outpouring, so much so that even after many had left the worship and thanksgiving started all over again.

Pam and I suddenly realised that the conference was not finishing until Sunday night and our flights were leaving Washington DC Sunday evening. We did not know how we would get to Washington DC on our own and we certainly would not manage on public transport. We had a problem, but we knew we had an amazing problem-solving God. Again, our prayer is always Lord let us be in the right place, at the right time, with the right people, doing the right thing. God was positioning us for breakthrough, and we could not wait to see what He was about to do!

Our hosts announced that they would be taking us on a tour of the Washington DC Monuments on Friday. Wow, that was an amazing answer to prayer for transportation for us! Pam and I planned to go on the tour bus with all our luggage, and then we could find some accommodation in Washington DC until we were due to depart on Sunday. Now all we needed was somewhere to stay.

Divine appointments

Seven months earlier, Hazel Dykins, Norma Dean, Pam Shaw and I had attended the European Parliament Prayer Breakfast in Brussels as we often had before. As we arrived, we were all given name badges but for some reason they had made a mistake with mine and I had become Sue Sinclair MEP (Member of the European Parliament). Sadly, that did not come with the salary or the MEP expenses! However, we had some fun with it! We were allocated specific tables to sit at, rather like when you are guests at a wedding. We found our table laid out beautifully for eight people and we got ourselves comfortable ready in anticipation to see who the other guests would be. I had a sneak peek: Ian and Jill Jeal were on one side and Mark and Karen Finlay were opposite them. I wondered who they were, and I was about to find out.

If you are in the right place, at the right time, doing the right thing, with the right people you are in position for a divine appointment! It was not long before we could hear a lovely Irish accent approaching and a couple settled at our table, introducing themselves as Mark and Karen Finlay. Mark announced that God had told them they were on the right table with the right people because he could sense the heavy anointing of God upon us. A few minutes later the table was completed as Ian and Jill Jeal sat down.

As soon as the worship, prayers and main speaker had finished, I began to prophesy over Mark and he laughed in shock and confirmation as he recognised that the Lord was speaking clearly to him. We all chatted happily sharing who we were, where we were from and what we were involved with and we exchanged business cards. We were supposed to go on to workshops which were located in other parts of the European Parliament building but we were so deep in conversation we forgot about them entirely. However, we knew that we were where God wanted us to be. Mark and Karen lived in Washington DC and were part of the team who facilitate the American Prayer Breakfast. We had an interesting conversation with Ian and Jill Jeal who lead prayer in the European Parliament when it is based in Strasbourg, France and warmly invited us there to pray.

Fast forward to just a few weeks before we flew out to Washington DC, Mark contacted me to say he wanted to talk to me about the prophetic word as it was starting to come to pass. I messaged him to let him know that we were coming to Washington DC and it would be great to see them again.

As soon as I knew we were going to need accommodation in Washington DC, I called Mark to see if he could recommend anywhere. Mark was keen to spend time with us and kindly arranged for us to stay at The Cedars in Arlington. Mark also managed to arrange for us to visit the White House whilst we were there! As you can imagine we could not wait!

EMBRACE IN WASHINGTON DC

On Friday we finished our time in Franklin and had a wonderful time on the Washington DC Monument tour. I especially loved the Abraham Lincoln Monument and would have appreciated more time there. Eventually it was time for us to step off the tour bus with our suitcases, and we were teary eyed as we said goodbye to everyone who had become such good friends to us.

We stepped out on to the hot street a little overwhelmed as we were now on our own in Washington DC. What did God have in store for us? Mark had given us an address to meet him at, so we climbed into a yellow cab and it was not too long before we arrived at one of the imposing government buildings near to the Capital Building. It was so good to connect with Mark again and we really enjoyed catching up as he drove us to the Cedars. We were overwhelmed as we arrived at our home for the next couple of days and knew we were in for an interesting time.

We were thrilled to stay in such a beautiful house full of incredible history. My eyes were drawn to the polished sideboard right opposite the front door in the elegant entrance hall. There on the top was a bronze model called "Embrace" a miniature of the three bronze sculptures, created as part of Liverpool's journey of apology and reconciliation regarding the transatlantic slave trade. An inscription on the base of the sculptures says, "Acknowledge the past, embrace the present, shape a future of reconciliation and justice". I love those life-shaping words!

I asked when did Lord David Alton visit? Mark was shocked that I knew he had been there, I explained the story of the Embrace sculptures located in Virginia, Benin and Liverpool.

Saturday morning Mark and Karen took us on a tour of some other parts of Washington DC, including the incredible Capital Building. It was great to be able to pray once again in these very strategic locations. Next, we joined the queue to go into the White House gardens. It was hilarious for me with my Liverpool sense of humour, as dotted about the area were several secret service agents. I know you are wondering how I knew they were secret service agents. Was it because I had prophetic revelation? No, they had "SECRET SERVICE" emblazoned in big letters all over their chests and on their backs! They were not very secret!

We loved the tour and took lots of photographs. As we got to the President's back door, I asked this lovely gentleman if he would take a photograph of Pam, Mark, Karen and myself. As I listened to his accent, I recognised that he was not American and asked him where he was from. We were all completely shocked when he said, "I am from Benin".

The image of the "Embrace" sculpture flashed back in my mind, as I asked him if he would allow us to pray for him and to bless Benin. Two Liverpool people, who had just come from Virginia, standing at President Obama's back door in the White House praying for Benin! Only God could arrange this incredible divine appointment and it was a powerful time of extravagant breakthrough being released for Liverpool, Benin, Virginia and the complete Transatlantic Slave Triangle.

It is so good to be in the right place, at the right time, with the right people, doing the right thing as it always releases heaven to earth! We enjoyed the rest of our time in Washington DC and returned home Sunday evening.

PRAYER: Thank you Jesus for the divine appointments you have in store for me. Help me to be in the right place, at the right time, with the right people, doing the right thing, alert and ready to respond when the opportunities arise. Help me to be a vessel of blessing who brings heaven to earth and lives to bring you glory. Amen.

Releasing The Mantles

Rwanda 2016

One step always leads to the next and it was our trip to South Africa as Alfie Fabe's guest that opened the door to Franklin in Virginia. Here we met the incredible Apostle Moses Kakungulu, who opened the door to Rwanda! We kept in touch with Moses and accepted his generous invitation to visit their church, the next time we visited neighbouring Uganda.

Our first trip in 2016 was amazing, although it was only for three days. Hazel Dykins and I ministered in the Prayer Palace Church, located in a large rented building. Everyone appeared so serious and sad as though they were not allowed to smile. I assumed that was because of the horrific genocide when 800,000 men, women and children had been slaughtered in just one hundred days in 1994. This shocking slaughter happened in our lifetime, and we were meeting so many precious people who had survived, while their whole families had been annihilated.

Before we flew out to Rwanda, the Lord gave me clear instructions to purchase beautiful deep blood red voile fabric. Having bought the voile, he described exactly how I was to make mantles, which we would use as He directed us. As we were leaving for church that first morning, the Lord told me to put two of the mantles in my bag. The worship time was so heavy, and the people were very serious. As I spoke there were no smiles or signs of encouragement, not at all like the very vocal Ugandans that we were used to.

When I had finished speaking, the Lord told me to call Apostle Moses and his wife up on to the platform. This beautiful gentle and humble couple stepped up on to the platform, and I explained to them and the congregation, that God had brought us to Rwanda to give them new mantles. These mantles represented the fresh authority, favour, leadership, and anointing God was releasing to them. God's presence was heavy, as Hazel and I placed the mantles around their shoulders and anointed them both with oil. Moses' head was dropped low but as he lifted it to look up at me, his big brown eyes filled up with huge tears that spilled over and flowed down his cheeks. Neither of them spoke a single word and there was a silent awe across the whole congregation.

Without knowing anything about the past, the Lord had led us to hit the target prophetically several times which massively impacted the future of this church bringing incredible and extravagant breakthrough! Moses took Hazel and I straight from church to a lovely restaurant for lunch. As we ate together Moses began to tell us his story . . .

The Prayer Palace Church was led by an incredible pastor, who birthed the church from nothing and was loved by everyone who knew her. Eight years earlier, she began to prepare to transfer the church leadership over to a young man called Moses. Although he was very young, God had also spoken to Moses and said, "He would be with him". The Pastor had decided that in one month's time she would hand her mantle over to Moses in front of the whole congregation and that way they would all know that the Lord had shown her that he was the best man to lead the church in the days ahead. Everything was planned between them, however a few days before this time of transition was to start, she suddenly died!

Moses was deeply shocked and traumatised, as this woman had been his spiritual mother as well as his pastor. Suddenly he found himself leading a broken-hearted church without the promised "mantle". Over the eight years since that time Moses had done his best to lead the church, although many people opposed his leadership. They did not know that their previous pastor had been preparing Moses to receive the leadership mantle once she stepped down.

For eight years Moses had struggled with his own grief whilst battling to stand against the control and manipulation of those hostile to him in the church. Many times, he had felt like giving up, but God would not allow him to. Praise God that He sent Hazel and I with mantles of leadership for him and his wife. God was publicly honouring Moses and acknowledging that He had chosen him to lead the church.

Later, Hazel and I visited the Presidential Palace where the first two Presidents of Rwanda had lived. The first elected President, Gregoire Kayibanda led the Rwandese struggle for independence from Belgium and replaced the Tutsi monarchy with a republican government. We saw the eerie remains of the plane, shot down into the grounds of the Palace, as it was approaching Kigali Airport nearby, on the evening of 6th April 1994. Everyone was killed, including the second President Juvenal Habyarimana and the President of Burundi, Cyprien Ntaryamira, plus all their staff. The Tour Guide told us that President Juvenal's wife immediately plotted the Genocide which started just 24 hours later!

If you are not in unity you will fall apart

We were collected from the Presidential Palace and taken to the building site of the new Prayer Palace Church not too far away. Moses and the Leadership Team had invited us to anoint their new building. It was a huge construction project and you could see the incredible potential. However, we knew that unless the church moved into the building in unity, it was not going to be fruitful. It was difficult, as we knew they were simply expecting us to worship with them and then anoint the building. However, I could hear God speaking very clearly, “I'm building my church with living stones and if you are not in unity it will fall apart”.

I knew God wanted to deal with the issues and heartbreak, so I took a big deep breath and challenged everyone to deal with any disunity. It was time for people to repent and to forgive one another. I looked around for something practical to help and spotted a long piece of wood which we dragged to the centre of the area that would eventually be the main worship sanctuary. We assembled everyone on one side, whilst Hazel and I stepped across to the other side. I shared what had happened that morning and how God had mantled Apostle Moses afresh for this new season. I then challenged them and encouraged people when they were in unity with Apostle Moses and each other, to step across the line.

Nothing happened! Nobody moved or prayed! I cried out to God, “Help!” By now it was starting to get dark and, with no lights, I was afraid we would not be able to see each other. I encouraged them again and a few minutes later people began to speak to one another and then started moving. One by one they stepped over the line, weeping, hugging one another and thanking God for what He was doing. We anointed them all as a sign of the fresh new start. There was great rejoicing as it began to rain as in 2 Chronicles 7:13-14 once again.

Extravagant breakthrough had come as a result of their obedience and a whole new season had started for Prayer Palace Church. We were so pleased to be able to give God the glory for all that He did that day. We counted it as a real privilege to be able to serve during those amazing few days in Rwanda and certainly left our hearts there.

PRAYER: Heavenly Father I invite you to show me any areas of disunity in my heart, that cause me to be divided from the rest of your body. Please help me to repent where I need to, forgive other people and myself where I need to. Help me to be positioned where you want me to be so I can be used by you to bring you glory. Amen.

Chaotic Roads And Flat Tyres

Uganda 2016

After a short flight from Rwanda to Entebbe Airport and a horrendous, very hot sweaty three-hour drive through the heaviest traffic you can imagine, Hazel and I arrived at our hotel. Hazel and I shared a room which turned out to be a lifesaver for me! I was desperate for a nice shower before our evening meal, so I quickly jumped in the shower cubicle. I slid the door across, moments later I was loving the refreshing water pouring over me. Ready for getting dried off, I reached out for the handle and panic set in! There was no internal handle and, try as I might, I could not open the door. Thankfully, I had not locked the bathroom door, so I shouted to Hazel, who quickly ran in to open the door for me from the outside. I thank God for Hazel or I may have still been stuck there!

We love Uganda and we have been partnering with our precious friend Arnold Muwonge for over twenty years now. We have been serving the Kampala Children's Centre (KCC) since 2005 and made our first visit in 2007. Since then, we have taken forty volunteers there as part of nine different teams. You can read some of the incredible stories from our trips there in my book Extravagant Adventures.

It has been wonderful to see the remarkable work at KCC developing and the children growing. Alongside that, over the years we have observed the work of the church leaders' network, Nations Disciple Enterprise (NDE) expanding on a large scale too. Every one of our trips has been a mixture of time at KCC with the children and staff, as well as serving the leaders at their churches and conferences. Our trips were always very busy!

Some days are grace opportunities, and this was one of those days! Prayer is essential when you are travelling overseas and especially on chaotic roads. Prayer has literally fuelled vehicles when the fuel tanks have been completely empty. Prayer has kept us safe when tyres have gone flat in the middle of an area full of lions. Once again, as people were praying for us, the Lord's protection for Hazel and I was incredible. This time we were driving to Pastor John Kisiita's church when, in the midst of busy traffic, we saw a driver in the next vehicle looking at us anxiously and pointing to our rear wheel. Thankfully, we were able to immediately pull straight into a garage. As we jumped out of the car, we were shocked to see the tyre was completely flat! Mercifully, it was fixed in a few minutes. Thank you, Jesus!

We were thrilled that we were able to minister again at Pastor John Kasiita's church with our friend John Kearns. John Kasiita was the first pastor we met in Uganda when we ministered in his church in 2007. You really need to read the story in *Extravagant Adventures*! The Ugandans struggle with my name and when they pronounce Sue, it sounds just like "shoe". 2007 was our very first visit to a Ugandan church and when they called me forward it sounded like "Pass the shoe!" Not understanding the Ugandan culture, I thought it may have been a strange way of taking the offering and whose shoe would they use? I still giggle when I think of "Pass the shoe!"

Our friend John Kearns preached an incredible message on Jesus' death and resurrection. I then ministered and invited the Holy Spirit to come, He came powerfully right into the building and gently blew around us all. In the afternoon both John and I preached again, with Hazel helping in prayer ministry and the response from the leaders was wonderful.

On Saturday Hazel and I were driven for about an hour to a well-constructed church full of hundreds of leaders. I preached for over two hours and it was a powerful time as people received from the Lord. We were then driven for a further hour to meet with precious leaders in a very humble village church which was still very much under construction! We had a wonderful time with these amazing people, so hungry and joyful to receive God's word.

On Sunday, once again we were so thankful for the prayers of our team at home! Hazel and I were guest speakers at Pastor Frank and Deborah's church. It was so good to be with them again and to see how both the children and the church have grown. As Frank was driving us all back to our hotel, his car ran out of fuel just as he was driving around the dangerous and very chaotic roundabout near to our hotel! There is a sign over the roundabout that says, "1.25 million people die per year on the roads, 90% of those are in the undeveloped world". The way that people drive there, that is really no surprise at all! We never take God's protection for granted and we are forever grateful for arriving safely at our destinations.

The following day we enjoyed our time at KCC exploring the new hospital that is under construction at the perimeter of the site. We were completely overwhelmed at this remarkable project which will be life-transforming for this community. We had a wonderful day with so much joy and laughter with the staff and children.

Wednesday evening was a special time for us as Moses flew in from Rwanda to join us for a meal. It certainly was a very precious time for us all.

Breakfast challenges

Arnold arranged a church and civic leaders prayer breakfast on Saturday morning, due to start at 9am. The Lord woke me at 5.30am to pray and prepare a strong word for them. I was desperate to deliver this word with God's love, power and anointing. We were there nice and early with Arnold and the band, as they were doing their final rehearsals. The hotel hosting the breakfast had decorated the tents so beautifully with tables and chairs all laid out, there was just one thing missing – the leaders. The civic leaders arrived on time but there was no sign of the church leaders. 9am came and went, 9.30am came and went, 10am came and went with a few leaders beginning to arrive. 10.30am came with a few more leaders arriving and on it went until at 11.30am the MC for the morning started the proceedings by thanking everyone for arriving on time!!!! What!!!! Really!!! Our Prayer Breakfast had turned into a Prayer Lunch!

There was a good time of worship and words of encouragement from some of the civic leaders before I was invited to speak. I started by honouring our friend Arnold and the civic leaders, then I began! I challenged the church leaders asking them if they were in a paid secular job would it be acceptable for them to arrive late. If they were one hour late or more would they be paid for their job or would they even have a job? I encouraged them that it was time for them to have a change of mindset and to honour God's presence and the civic leaders by being on time. I received a round of applause from the chief of police who came across to shake my hand when I had finished speaking. Sometimes we need to challenge and change the accepted norm if we are looking to see breakthrough come. It ended up being a powerful time as God moved in our midst.

Arnold was driving us back to KCC when the sky that had become very heavy and black began to release the full weight of a very serious storm upon us. The roads were instantly flooded as torrents of heavy rain poured down upon us, turning the bumpy dirt roads into deep muddy rivers. We were surrounded by loud rumbles of thunder that filled the whole atmosphere and the sky was violently bursting with huge flashes of lightening, forking in every direction. The window wipers on Arnold's car were wiping extra fast but could not keep the screen clear. Then, as suddenly as it all came, the storm stopped, and it was not long before the sun was shining brightly again.

Spirit of joy breaks out

Back at KCC again, we assembled with all the staff and children in one of the large workshops located between Abundant House and New Beginnings. (These are two of the homes that we had raised the money to build). We had an incredible time of praise and worship with such freedom and love as everyone focussed their eyes upon Jesus. It was our joy then to bless our wonderful friend Arnold with one of the beautiful mantles we had brought. As we wrapped the mantle around his shoulders and began to pray, the power of God fell heavily upon Arnold and a real spirit of joy cascaded down upon us all.

Our last day at KCC was marked by lots of happy tears and surprises. Then it was time for us to leave. Arnold and the children prayed for us before Patrick drove us back to our accommodation. On the way it was a great blessing for us to spot two crested cranes in the marshes at the side of the road. We had never seen them before. Even though they are the national bird of Uganda they are not seen very often. Again, we thank God for all that He has done.

PRAYER: Dear heavenly Father I ask that you reveal any strongholds I have in my thinking which prevent you moving in power in my life and through my life. I ask you to bring breakthrough in every area, that I may live to bring you glory. Amen.

Mantles Of Breakthrough

Rwanda 2018

2018 was our second trip to Rwanda. Hazel and I were pleased to be joined by Angela and Ann this time. We arrived after a very long journey and it was not long before we settled into our new home for the next week. We were staying in a beautiful house belonging to Janet, an incredible businesswoman involved with mining and hospitality. Janet's Auntie Dorothy lives in the house and is a courageous 78-year-old lady who was in charge of caring for us. Auntie Dorothy only spoke French and we all only spoke English, so that was a challenge. However, we quickly discovered that love and hugs communicate across all language barriers.

During our first afternoon we ministered at the National Prayer Altar led by Pastor Frank, which was located on the fourth floor of a building with no lift and a lot of uneven dangerous stairs! It was great to be there, and I spoke on Elijah over the next three days, which was very well-received. We were pleased to have an opportunity to pray with everyone who came.

That evening we ministered in the Prayer Palace Church. Hazel and I were amazed as we arrived at the church, which was simply a construction site last time we visited. Now ready for growth, the church quickly filled up with beautiful smiley people. We loved the worship – even though we did not always understand the language of the worship songs, we knew God was smiling too. Patrick was leading the worship which was incredible, and I was pleased that he was also my interpreter, as we flowed so well together. I could speak confidently knowing that Patrick was keeping up with me and we were communicating the same message. (I have to say that is not always the case!) We were invited to Patrick's home where each Thursday evening they watch a live stream of revival meetings attended by 50,000 people in Kampala, Uganda. It was not long before their home was full of people hungry for God and we had a great evening together.

Weeping with those who weep

Early the next day we visited the Kigali Genocide Museum. Despite Hazel and I having visited this museum before, we were still so shocked by what we saw. It is truly shocking that this happened in front of the eyes of the world, less than three decades ago. Sadly, nothing ever prepares you for what man is actually capable of doing or the scale of this horrific genocide that resulted in the deaths of over a million people. But death was not the only outcome as tens of thousands of people were tortured and mutilated, suffering horrific machete cuts, bullet wounds, infections and starvation. Many thousands were widowed, many were raped and sexually abused or tortured by seeing their children brutally murdered. There were over 300,000 children orphaned, and we saw terrible images of little children whose heads had been caved in with machetes as whole families were completely wiped out. We saw a photograph of a beautiful two-year-old little girl with the most beautiful huge brown eyes, but they stabbed her in the eyes until she died!

We visited the mass graves where at least 250,000 people are buried. We heard that bodies are still being discovered and being buried there. We met a precious woman who had lost her whole family and although we did not speak the same language, we immediately connected with her. Hugs speak love in any language! She took us to where her family were buried, and we cried and prayed with her. She eagerly found someone to interpret for us all so she could thank us.

We cried many tears there and felt deep shock at man's depravity to man. We know that we are ministering in Rwanda to help in the recovery and healing but only God can heal these broken and traumatised hearts.

Later that day, we moved on to the National Prayer Altar for our final session, with a greater appreciation of what these precious people have endured. What an amazing afternoon. We knew we were full of God's power as we delivered His word about trusting again. We had to be really direct, even though it was very difficult to talk about, as the Rwandan people are clearly still healing from the Genocide.

We had a powerful time; everyone was of one mind and heart, ready to pray for a shift and breakthrough for Rwanda. We constructed a Prayer Altar together with the names of churches and ministries written upon them. Everyone participated by praying, repenting, forgiving, and blessing. We gave everyone an opportunity to come and pray directly over the Prayer Altar before we stood together to bless the church in Rwanda. Patrick and the worship team began to lead us all in praise and thanksgiving, when suddenly Ann began to dance. Ann was so anointed, and she brought such a sense of breakthrough. We cannot wait to see what happens next!

Sunday morning, we returned to the Prayer Palace Church to minister at their morning service. Wow, God moved powerfully!! I preached a message on "The Lamb of God". The whole team participated, and we were well-received with many people responding to the message. Angela brought a word and prayed a blessing over all the children.

It was soon time to say our "Goodbyes" to those who had welcomed us so warmly. It was hard leaving Auntie Dorothy whom we had all grown to love so much. The language barrier had not improved very much but we departed with a deep love in our hearts for each other. I called her my Rwandan Mama and she called me her Rwandan daughter; so powerful when we knew she had lost her children in the slaughter.

We were dropped at Kigali Airport ready for our one-hour flight to Uganda and the start of our week based at KCC. At the airport we encountered a beautiful family who were leaving for New Zealand and I had an opportunity to pray for them all before they said their farewells to the rest of their family.

PRAYER: Heavenly Father I bring the people of Rwanda to you and ask that you will continue to bring reconciliation and healing to them. I pray that I will be a person who always brings peace wherever you lead me. Amen.

Demolishing The Church

Uganda 2018

Over the years we have taken over forty people from ages 17 to 79 to Uganda, whose lives have been massively impacted by their experiences. These trips have continued to develop our friendship with Arnold, all at KCC and many leaders. Hazel and Ann had been several times, however this trip to Uganda 2018 was Angela's first trip.

We could not wait to see Patrick again as he always drives us, and we particularly appreciate his amazing ability to navigate the busy and chaotic traffic of Kampala. It was incredible to see the children of KCC again and it is always a shock to see how much they have grown. We have known many of them since they were tiny, particularly those who have lived in our home Abundant House. Most of them are teenagers now and studying hard, preparing for University or College.

We always have a "wow" moment when we arrive at KCC again, as it is all so stunningly beautiful, peaceful and full of life. Every time we return, we witness the new developments and growth – always so much growth! We spent the day exploring and chatting with the children and young people. What a joy! Thank you, Jesus, for this incredible privilege.

Later we were driven to Wakiso, which is the nearest town to KCC and now the home of Destiny Bridge City Church (Arnold's church). They used to meet in a small wooden building in the grounds of KCC, which also doubled as the school, but they quickly outgrew that. Now that tiny little school at KCC has been replaced by three modern school buildings providing education for hundreds of children from both KCC and the community.

Prophecy, healing and breakthrough

Destiny Bridge City Church was a humble building, full of life and energy. By the time we arrived for the "Prophecy, Healing and Breakthrough Conference" the worship was well under way and there was such a sense of excitement and anticipation. The church was full of people of all ages, with many familiar faces including pastors and leaders from other churches across the region.

I was thrilled to see Pastor Fire and his family who I had not seen for several years. I remembered the first time I had encountered Pastor Fire at one of Arnold's Conferences. He was down on his knees crying out to God in deep intercession with such hunger and desperation. I remember saying to Arnold, "What an amazing name Pastor Fire!" Arnold told me it was not his real name but the African name he had chosen for himself. Arnold asked me if I wanted an African name. As soon as I said, "Yes" he instantly responded, "You are called Anointed for Breakthrough!" That was many years ago and since then we have seen many incredible breakthroughs.

Herbert and one of KCC's worship teams led the beautiful worship. It was wonderful to see these amazing little children, now grown and helping to lead worship so powerfully. I could not stop thanking God for them all.

From the first evening Arnold and I flowed together powerfully with the Holy Spirit. I spoke on the story of Elijah over the three evenings and shared prophetically about what had happened in Liverpool on 31st December 2017. OpenWell (the church I attend) had met in a school building as usual, only what was unusual was that a prop from the school's Christmas pantomime had been left behind. It was the front half of a little red car with no steering wheel and the registration plate JLKI. My eyes were drawn straight to it and the Lord said, "The registration JLKI stood for Jesus Loves Kingdom Initiatives. 2018 will mark the start of a shift of the way many of us will do church. There will be a return to the Gospel as the foundation and a restoration of signs, wonders and miracles".

Later, OpenWell gathered with Victory Outreach Church near to the Albert Docks for a joint New Years' Eve party. As we got close the whole atmosphere became full of very thick black smoke, and it was not long before we heard the news that there was a huge fire in The Liverpool Echo Arena car park. Eight hours before the start of the New Year, a fire had started in a sixteen-year-old Land Rover on the third floor of the car park. The fire had quickly spread throughout the whole car park. It had taken only eight minutes for the fire brigade to get to the car park but sixteen hundred vehicles were destroyed as the car park was full.

As we worshipped later in the evening, the Lord explained to me that cars speak prophetically about ministry. Sixteen hundred cars had been destroyed by the fire and He was clearing many of our ministries from the old season to make way for a return to "Jesus' Love Kingdom Initiatives" that will be fire-fuelled and manifesting miracles.

It was eight hours before the start of new year 2018, eight minutes before the fire brigade arrived, a fault in a sixteen-year-old Land Rover that started the fire and 1600 cars destroyed. These are all multiples of eight that biblically means new beginnings! I knew God was saying, He was about to move very powerfully in Liverpool and through Liverpool to the nation and nations, releasing new beginnings complete with signs, wonders and miracles. People who had locked up their cars, would now hopefully have new cars with new keys. God was saying, "I am asking you to lock up the old things that are no longer fruitful for this new season. For I am about to release new keys with an upgrade for your ministries".

A week later, I noticed the little red car was still there on the platform and I heard the Lord say, "There is no steering wheel for you to use because I want to lead the way in this season". The question for us all is, will we allow the Lord to steer us?

BREAKING THE GLASS CEILING

Back to my talk in Uganda, I continued by speaking of our precious friend Julie Wickenden (who has been there many times) and shared the story of how I had prophesied about the "Glass ceiling".

I will let Julie tell the story:

"In July 2014 Sue and a small team from CWM came to encourage us. We went to Tehilla Prayer House with Honor to share our dreams and for the CWM team to pray a commissioning blessing over the Prayer House. It was a powerful time and at one-point Sue launched into a significant prayer that all those who had felt restricted (especially women), by others would be released into the fullness of their ministries and callings, and that the "glass ceiling would be shattered". This was so poignant and powerful as both Honor and I had felt that reaching our destinies in God had been hampered by misunderstanding, lack of meaningful support, and even suspicion from leaders in many of the churches we had aimed to serve over the years. When Sue and team pray prayers like that under the direction of the Holy Spirit, watch out!

As we left Tehilla House to take the short walk back to Honor's house, I noticed missed calls on my mobile phone. My daughter had been frantically calling to tell me that the ceiling of our dining room had suddenly collapsed, around the time that Sue had prayed! It was dramatic. It was messy. It was real! I love it when God confirms His word with a visible demonstration of His power. Since that day, Honor and I have certainly felt more boldness and confidence in our unique callings, and with renewed respect from those around us, doors of opportunity have continued to open in the most unusual places. Be encouraged: "God's gifts and God's call are under full warranty – never cancelled, never rescinded" (Romans 11:29).

Back to Uganda: I shared that God was saying that for many glass ceilings were about to come down. However, there was a hinderance to God really moving powerfully – the church leaders were divided and in disunity, they were competing against one another, they were jealous and intimidated by one another. God said, "Their disunity is holding back a move of My Spirit!" God was calling them to repent and to bring down their walls of division.

Old things needed to be locked up so that God could release the new keys of authority for the season of new beginnings, which was already starting. I presented Arnold with a new key (I did not know that he had been asking the Lord for a new key!) and we invited all the pastors and leaders to come to the front. I handed the microphone over to one of the pastors who began to lead a powerful time of repentance, crying out to God, full of sorrow for their disunity and pride.

When they had finished, we called on God to bring down the walls of division and disunity. Arnold followed through, bringing an anointed word about breaking down the walls of Jericho! He declared a breaking off of all chains of repression, the place erupted and there was lots of dancing! The Holy Spirit powerfully flooded the place! The Lord showed Angela a vision of the walls coming down as the leaders were repenting and it definitely felt like there was a shift! Little did we know!!

SURPRISE, SURPRISE!

We had lunch with Arnold on Thursday whilst everyone else was busy preparing a surprise party for Ann. Ann was having a special birthday this year and we all wanted to celebrate, but we just had not told her. She and Hazel had no clue! When three of the littlest children came to collect us in their best dresses and escort us to the party, Ann still had no clue!

The little ones escorted us through a tunnel of love formed by the children and staff, who threw beautiful pink petals over us as we ran through. They honoured us all as we were led to four seats under a thatched canopy. All the trees in the garden were decorated with multicoloured balloons, with chairs laid out in neat rows underneath. In the centre was a huge beautifully decorated cake. All the children and young people living in KCC were there and Ann still had no clue this was all for her!

The children sang, danced and made speeches, suddenly Ann realised this was all in her honour for the start of her 80th year! Many of the children gave thanks to our CWM Team for building their homes. Susan said she would not have been alive today but for our help! It was so humbling for us, as we all wept tears of joy. It reminded us again of the importance of this life changing ministry that God has called us to support. There was lots more dancing and party poppers before Arnold and the children prayed for Ann. The children helped Ann to blow out the candles on her huge birthday cake, before it was sliced up for everyone to enjoy.

The next day we started early before it got too hot to climb to the top of Destiny Hill, just behind KCC. There is a wonderful view of the whole region, and it is certainly a great place to pray. There were several people already there, tucked under trees praying and spending time with God. Hazel had struggled with her knee and one of the men on the top had spotted that Hazel was in pain. He came over, introduced himself as Pastor Joseph and offered to pray for her. Pastor Joseph prayed with such fervour before he escorted us back down towards KCC. On the way down he offered to give me his children! Shocking but true! We introduced him to Arnold to see if they could help.

When we arrived back at KCC we had some quality time with the little ones. What a joy!!! Hazel had made them some beautiful teddies and animals. The children made lots of little speeches, welcoming us into their home. So cute!! Then the older boys invited us into New Beginnings House, escorting us around their immaculate rooms with great pride. Next the music went on and they started dancing for us. Wow!!! Many of them made speeches thanking us for their home and all that has been provided for them. We were so emotional and overjoyed at all God is doing in their lives.

Next, we visited the new hospital located at the entrance of KCC. From one side it still looked like a construction site but on the other it is so beautiful. All we could say as Nurse Edith proudly showed us around was "Wow!!!!!". Arnold really is one of the most incredible apostolic pioneers who is making a difference to so many people's lives.

Friday morning Arnold walked up to the top of KCC with us, to see the foundations for the new school. The builders spotted the "Muzungu women" (white women) and moments later we all had proposals from the workmen who were looking for white women to marry! We told them we were not looking for husbands in Uganda, as we were in love with Jesus and our husbands back home. They were all Muslims, so we were pleased to have an opportunity to talk to them and pray for them.

TOO DANGEROUS TO USE

Saturday morning, we ministered at a Leaders' Breakfast, and everyone was really attentive as Arnold and I spoke. I spoke first from John 10 about the sheep recognising the voice of the shepherd and him coming to lead them out. I encouraged the leaders to empower their people to hear the voice of the shepherd, so they could follow Him out of the church buildings in the days ahead.

Arnold spoke after me and as he was speaking his phone began to ping repeatedly as messages were coming in. He apologised and quickly checked his phone. Arnold looked across at me a little surprised, as he announced that his church had just collapsed and then just carried on sharing! I thought he was joking, as I cannot imagine any other leader would get a message like that and just carry on speaking!

However, it was not long before a photo arrived showing that the roof and ceiling had totally collapsed into the church. Huge wooden beams had simply broken in half and we were told that the walls had huge cracks in them too, rendering the church building completely unsafe to use! Two days after we had prophesied about the ceiling coming down, walls of disunity coming down and old things being locked up – the church building was rendered too dangerous to use.

Arnold was busy with his team for the rest of the day, arranging for all the PA equipment and instruments to be removed from the church building as quickly and safely as possible. Church members were running around ordering marquees and everything necessary to host God's presence in a church without walls.

Sunday dawned, a beautiful morning and we were really excited! There was such a sense that God was going to do something very special. We arrived at KCC where they had erected three large marquees in the field. Arnold was sitting in the gates welcoming everyone as they arrived, and the worship team were already mid-flow really enjoying God's presence. It was incredible to see what Destiny Bridge City Church had achieved in less than twenty-four hours.

I was filled with huge anticipation as I could sense the expansion and breakthrough as people were being transported from the original church building in the village. The worship was wonderful and the atmosphere electric. Arnold spoke, giving a review of what had happened and a stirring challenge to the church for the days ahead.

I spoke, recapping what God had said prophetically throughout the Conference a few days earlier:

1) God is calling us to lock up the old so that we can receive the new keys for this new season.
2) God wants to be at the steering wheel of our lives.
3) Walls of disunity have been broken down so that the Bride of Christ can now emerge.
4) God is calling us all to watch as He extends our personal tent pegs. For He is going to stretch us way beyond what we can naturally do. Be ready! Watch! Step up, step out and step into our anointing for God is about to take us to another level and another expansion of territory. We will see some significant breakthroughs!
5) God is bringing the ceilings down!

We had such a powerful time together as God ministered and we were pleased to be there at such a time of change. It had been an incredible and profound trip and we give glory to God for all the amazing things He has done.

PRAYER: Heavenly Father I give you the steering wheel of my life and I ask you to break any glass ceilings over me that have contained or confined me. I am ready for you to stretch me and I look forward to seeing where you lead me in the days ahead. I thank you that you will give me everything I need to fulfil the call you have put upon my life and I choose to live to glorify you. Amen.

The Gift Of Keys

Ghana 2016

We had known Maria Akrofi for a little while as she lives in Liverpool and had been coming to the Big PUSH. We could see she was an incredible woman of God and we instantly loved her. Maria asked if I would pray for her husband Justice. I was thrilled to meet him, and God gave me a huge prophetic word for him. I came away wondering who on earth this unassuming, humble and gentle man was. A few days later we discovered he was the recently retired Archbishop of West Africa!!

For some years I had known God was calling me to go to Ghana and when we were invited by Maria and Justice, we knew it was a divine appointment to go. Pam and I were struggling to get our visas through in time for our trip in 2016; however, thanks to Maria's intervention, the Ghanaian Ambassador to the UN contacted the Embassy in London on our behalf. We thanked God for His favour and for the adventures that lay ahead.

Our arrival at Kotoka Airport in Ghana was a challenge. Pam struggles a little with her mobility, so when we travel, we arrange for a wheelchair which makes the journey through the airports a lot easier. We got through passport control and all we had left to do was collect our luggage. That sounds easy right? No! It was dangerous chaos as I struggled to get our luggage amongst people pushing, shoving and elbowing everyone out of the way. Suitcases of all sizes were being flung and thrown around with complete disregard to anybody around them. I came out of the experience literally covered in bruises.

Our first day was a day of rest, and John (Justice and Maria's eldest son) invited us to a little prayer meeting at 11am. However, it was a bank holiday in Ghana, and we had not realized that the Empowerment Worship Centre was hosting twelve hours of worship, prayer and prophecy. We arrived as the amazing worship was in full flow and Pam and I naively believed we could slip into this meeting unnoticed, despite being the only white faces in the middle of hundreds of beautiful black faces. The Lord began to speak to me:

At the airport, there was a wrestling and a jostling for the baggage. God is saying, "It is time for you to release the baggage from the past season, so that you can be free to receive what I am releasing in this season".

As we worshipped, I could see the room full of white doves. I asked the Lord "What are they doing here?" The Lord said, "They are bringing peace and mighty breakthroughs. They are landing on those whose hearts are prepared and have released the baggage of the past." He wants you to carry the anointing for peace and breakthrough to those around you; to your families, your communities and your nation.

Those who are not willing to let go of the past will not receive what God is pouring out in this new season. So, let go . . . let go of the old tatty baggage and receive your upgrade.

I told the Lord that if He wanted me to share this word, He would need to make an opportunity for me to do that. As a visitor I was not going to march up to the front to bring a "Word". The worship finished and someone got up to preach a very passionate message that was certainly received very enthusiastically. Although Pam and I could not understand very much, we loved the atmosphere and the strong sense of God's presence. As the next session of worship began, we slipped out so we could meet Justice for lunch.

John stopped to refuel the car in the petrol station just around the corner. A few moments later, Prophet Gideon the leader of the Empowerment Worship Centre called wanting to meet us after he had noticed we had left. Gideon was waiting for us at the entrance of the church. As we chatted, he clearly recognised that we were carrying something powerful for them and thrust us on to the platform to release it. We felt a bit sorry for the guy who was mid-way through speaking, who was hurried off the stage as we were introduced.

I shared the word the Lord had given me, and it was received with great excitement. Gideon prayed powerfully for us before crouching down. He said that he felt like he needed to PUSH, as though he was about to give birth to something! Can you imagine the amazement for Pam and I as we were propelled from the car to the platform in front of a thousand people to receive such a reaction? And this was our day off! God was laughing!

Escaping exploding repellents

We always thank God for his divine protection and never take it for granted. The next day as we were just coming out of our hotel into the traffic, a Sasso van carrying very flammable insecticide, collided with another vehicle at the junction and lost control right into our lane! The van driver, panicking, quickly jumped out and with the help of a police officer desperately attempted to disconnect the battery. However, smoke was already pouring out of the van and it was clearly a very dangerous situation. Thankfully, the traffic lights changed in our favour, so our driver quickly sped through the junction getting us away from the danger. As we looked back, we watched the van explode and burst into a massive ball of flames! We later heard that some people close to the vehicle sustained various injuries resulting from the pressurised insecticide cans exploding. We knew that had we been a few seconds earlier or later we would have been very seriously injured.

BUILDING THE FOUNDATIONS FOR BREAKTHROUGH

We drove for almost three hours towards Cape Coast and the Elmina Slave Castle with Maria. We were almost there when Maria asked if we would like to visit the Bishop of Cape Coast. We said, "Yes because we actually have a gift for him". The Lord had told Pam and I to bring an ancient set of keys and He would tell us who to give them to. Maria was trying to decide if we should visit Bishop Victor on the way to Elmina or on the way back. I asked, "Can we go now?" A few minutes later Bishop Victor was welcoming us into his home and telling us we had arrived in perfect time, as he had been about to go out. Had we visited on the way back from Elmina we would have missed him! It is so good to be in the right place, at the right time, with the right people, doing the right thing!

We had a powerful time with Bishop Victor and his wife Dorcas, as we repented regarding Liverpool's role in the transatlantic slave trade. We prophesied over them and presented them with the ancient keys. God told us to give them £20, 20 Euros and 20 Ghanaian Cedes and we later realised that 20 in the Bible signifies Freedom! We explained that God wanted them to receive the keys as they were no longer to be orphan victims of the slave trade, but they needed to choose to be free as children of God. We encouraged them to ask the Lord, were there any things that they needed to repent of as Africans? Were there any ways that their ancestors had contributed to the slave trade? Little did we know what God was planning! It was time for them to arise into their destinies and to begin to pray in faith, knowing that God loved them and wanted to bless them.

DOOR OF NO RETURN

We then drove to the white-washed Elmina Slave Castle, which had a weird sense of incredible beauty from a distance and of hell on earth close up, all in the same place. Elmina is a very busy town, bursting with life as people struggle to make a living. As we drove into the bustling town centre, we spotted the street sign pointing to Liverpool Street, which made me feel sick, as it was clear evidence of Liverpool's horrible history. It felt very intimidating as we walked from the car to this UNESCO World Heritage site, with young men at the side of the road doing everything they could to sell us their wares. The Elmina Castle's ancient walls were once home to one of the most tragic and brutal periods of human history that lasted over three centuries. I felt the weight of the shame and pain enveloping me that my city was responsible for much of that.

We crossed the little footbridge over the moat to the entrance, to see and hear some of the horrific stories that were stored within. Our lovely guide unpacked the official tour, recounting stories of the brutal rapes of so many women, as well as the torture and death of many of those set aside for slavery. There are no words to describe this utter hell hole!

It was interesting that as we stood in the final slave cellar in front of the "Door of No Return" there was Pam and I from Liverpool, Maria plus our Tour Guide from Ghana and two Americans – symbolic of the Transatlantic Slave Triangle. It was a divine appointment and opportunity to pray not only about the past, but also about the modern-day slave crisis.

It was late when we arrived back to our hotel, however we had a nice surprise awaiting us. Evelyn had come to the Big PUSH in Liverpool several times when she lived in the UK as a student and had seen via Facebook that we were in Ghana. I had let her know where we were staying, and she had driven a three-hour round trip to visit us. She shared amazing testimonies of how the Big PUSH had impacted her life and we had a really precious time together.

CELEBRATING JUSTICE

Saturday was the main reason for our trip, the celebration of Archbishop Justice's forty years of priesthood. This included twenty years as Bishop of Ghana and Archbishop of West Africa, and Justice and Maria had decided to mark this special occasion by launching the Akrofi Foundation. The service was attended by many VIPs, clergy, family, and friends. The church was bursting with people there to honour Justice's ministry. The challenge for me, was that we had always known Justice simply as our precious friend and suddenly when the bishops and dignitaries were parading down the aisle I started to panic. There were bishops from many nations complete with all their robes, making their way down the aisle and right at the end was Justice. He was all robed up in beautiful gold vestments and his mitre, and as I saw Justice I just burst into tears. Help me Jesus, Justice is a real Archbishop!!!

Pam and I sat on the front row, which was terrifying, as there was nobody in front of us to show us what to do. We had no idea of the protocols, when to sit down or stand up, or bow or perform lots of the other traditions. It was a terrifying mystery and we were in the middle of it! I was due to speak after the Bishop of Cameroon and as I watched the other speakers, I just became more and more intimidated. Each person stood and knew when they needed to bow and how to address everyone with all the correct titles and there were lots of titles!!! Bishop Thomas took his place and had everyone singing and was totally amazing. I cried, "Please help me Jesus! Could you just make a hole in the ground to take me out of this?" The next moment it was my turn and I was still busy appealing to Jesus for help. As I looked up to the row of bishops sitting across the back of the altar, I saw Justice give me a huge smile and I heard the Lord speak, "Just be yourself". I rose to the lectern and took a deep breath.

I turned to the congregation and began to talk to them about my precious friend Justice. I read and unpacked Isaiah 61 which was one of Justice's favourite passages of scripture. I encouraged Justice by telling him that God wanted him to know that as he celebrated forty years, it was not a time of retirement, but he had only just passed his time of probation! Justice laughed, everyone cheered, and I thanked God that my shaking legs were still holding me up! Pam did really well, looking so confident as she shared a reading. The whole service was beautiful and lasted for four hours before Pam and I were warmly introduced to all of the bishops. We later spoke to Chief Justice Georgina Wood and arranged to meet her in her office a few days later. We continued the celebrations at a beautiful reception with over two hundred guests.

On Sunday we attended St Anthony's Church service with all of the Bishops and their wives who had stayed to continue the celebrations. This service only lasted three hours! However, for me there was one incredible moment as we took communion. Hundreds of people filed to the communion rail and fell to their knees to receive the bread and wine. As Justice was the guest of honour, he was the first person to receive communion and as I was his guest, I was next. I knelt next to Justice and as the huge silver cup of wine was passed to me, I realised how full it was. I held it carefully and bent over to take a sip when it happened – there in the dark red wine was the reflection of my face! My face looking up at me through Jesus' blood. The tears rolled down my face, as I realised once more the huge price that Jesus had paid for me, just because He loves me so much. Wow, thank you Jesus!

Later, back at our hotel, Pam and I were honoured to minister to some of the bishops and their wives privately. God moved very powerfully, and we were grateful to God for all He did.

Monday was the start of our five day "Prayer and Prophecy School" in St Anthony's Church. I spoke, followed by Pam who spoke brilliantly and then we both prayed for lots of people. The Holy Spirit came big style, moving very powerful and it was as though many had never encountered the Holy Spirit before! At least two ladies were physically healed, one of severe shoulder pain and the other of stomach pain. Praise God, several people were set free and many, including several of the clergy, were in floods of tears as God was filling them afresh with His love. They were so hungry and open to God.

The worship team were touched so powerfully by the Holy Spirit that they were struggling to keep standing and so other people had to step in to lead the worship, to keep the flow going! It was nothing to do with Pam or I, it was just God!

Positions of power to shocking discoveries

Our scheduled day off was an amazing day which began with a private meeting with the incredible Chief Justice Georgina Wood. God spoke to me to share the story of the Hillsborough disaster because of the similar terrible disaster in the Accra Stadium 9th May 2001 when 127 people died. Once again there had been no justice and a huge cover up that has been operating ever since. I challenged her to see if anything could be done to bring justice for those families and survivors.

We shared some verses with Chief Justice Georgina, and then she invited us to attend the official Justice Annual Church Service on Saturday morning plus the reception afterwards. I suddenly remembered a prophetic word that had been given to me a few months earlier that God had a divine appointment for me with a judge! This was certainly a divine appointment and we had a very powerful time. We paused to give God all the glory for what happened and for the outcome.

We visited many places and people, including a family who were friends of Maria who had just been bereaved. We had an hour of sweet worship and prayer with them, and sensed God's love pouring out everywhere we went.

We also witnessed the terrible sight of a dozen people parading from the Fetish Temple. To our horror, a little later we also witnessed a young woman stripped naked to the waist and daubed in white powder. She looked deranged as she marched speedily along the pavement with people pointing at her, mocking and laughing. Maria told us she was a slave given to the Fetish Temple by her family. I was grief-stricken for her and desperately wanted to stop the car to try to rescue her. Can you believe that families actually do this because they believe that it will break the power of curses over them? Young women are given as slaves and just about anything can happen to them including traumatic sexual abuse. This is clearly against the law here and yet it remains very much a part of the Ghanaian culture! It is shocking that a nation so impacted by the trauma of the transatlantic slave trade continues to turn a blind eye to these precious women because it is part of their culture! Society chooses to turn a blind eye to something for so long, that it is no longer seen as an atrocity against these girls and against God! God help us and them!

Favour of God

We were utterly overwhelmed at the goodness and favour of God through Maria and Justice. We met Dr Mary Chinery-Hessey who is one of the most utterly remarkable and influential women we have ever met. We had an hour meeting scheduled with her, however we were there for much longer! We were told to call her "Your Excellency" but she immediately put us at ease. As we introduced ourselves, she said "Please call me Mary". Mary is the most amazing, courageous and humble 78-year-old we have ever met. Mary loves Jesus and the stories she told us were incredible and unrepeatable for confidentiality purposes. We instantly loved Mary and we enjoyed a powerful prayer time together.

We were honoured to meet and pray with Rebecca and her close friend Shirley. Rebecca's husband Akufo Addo was running to be President of Ghana in the December elections. This was his third attempt after the two previous attempts had been difficult. We had a powerful time as God spoke right into Rebecca and Akufo's lives with such accuracy.

The evening brought the Prophecy School to an end and Pam and I had decided to finish with a fire tunnel, which was a whole new experience for everyone there. A fire tunnel is a powerful method of praying for lots of people, by forming a human tunnel of people standing opposite one another. They stretch out their hands towards each other to create the tunnel and people walk through receiving prayer as they go. For some they were thrown in at the deep end, as with Afua Ghantey and her friend who arrived half-way through the evening. Afua is a very powerful lady and she was deeply touched by God. As we finished, Pam and I were so honoured by their love and generosity as they presented us with so many beautiful gifts.

Dedicating the law year to God

Our final day was packed full of incredible moments from beginning to end. We attended the Annual Legal Service, which marks the start of the legal year in Ghana.The whole service at the cathedral was recorded live for national TV. The place was full, and we hoped we could slip in at the back. However, we were amazed to be escorted to seats very near to the front. Our new friends Chief Justice Georgina and Afua, had main parts to play in the service and they were amazing. It was an impactful Christian service and both these ladies in particular really gave glory to God in a big way.

Later, we attended the reception alongside five hundred VIPs at the front of the Law buildings. We had no clue where to sit but we bumped straight into Afua who presented us with more gifts before taking us right to the front row, nearest Georgina's seating. Everyone was invited to stand as Georgina's car complete with police escort arrived. We were very shocked when she stepped out of the car and came straight over to greet us!!! If that was not shocking enough, she whispered that she had a gift for us!! We were introduced to so many interesting people including David, a very senior police officer.

They had a wonderful Gospel choir singing and everyone enjoyed worshipping Jesus. It was not long before our new friend (the Chief Justice!) was climbing into her car, complete with the escort vehicles with sirens blaring she waved to us all and she was gone, disappearing into the busy traffic.

Wow what a trip! We had never had such powerful doors open, with such favour and so many opportunities. Glory to God for He opened the doors and gave us the words to speak that have clearly impacted and changed so many people's lives. We knew we had walked in the power released by the prayers of our team back home. We knew we had stepped through into another level with God and we give Him all the glory.

We celebrated that President Nana Akufo-Addo was sworn into office on 7th January 2017 and Rebecca became the First Lady. What a shift! Praise God for a Christian President!

PRAYER: Heavenly Father I thank you for what you can do when I make my life available to you. Today I declare I am willing to go wherever you want me to go and I thank you for the divine appointments you have ready for me to step into. Amen.

Restoration Amongst The Nations

April 2017

God has been ensuring that we have been in the right place, at the right time, with the right people, doing the right thing for heaven to come to earth and this trip was no different. 2017 was our second trip to Ghana, and we were pleased to be staying in the same hotel in Accra as before. Saturday morning, Pam and I woke early and had an incredible time with the Lord. He was so close as we cried out to Him for a move of His Spirit upon us and all those He had called us to minister to.

Maria arranged for us to provide some prayer and prophecy to a very influential leader. She arrived looking sad and overwhelmed, and thanks to Jesus she left very happy and encouraged. It was awesome watching her as God got to the heart of the matter in her life. Wow! We serve a mighty God!

Early Sunday morning we attended the main Anglican service at St Anthony's Church. It was a high church service and we found it very hard to follow but God's presence was so sweet. I had prepared a message and then the Lord told me earlier in the morning that I could not preach it! God told me I had to speak from my heart, and I prayed that I would glorify Him. I spoke from Isaiah 61 and related the stories of what God had been doing, as we believed His word and put it into action. There was a great response and we were humbled to be invited to pray with so many people when the service ended. We were honoured to pray and prophesy over the clergy and to watch as what we had prophesied came to pass in the coming months.

Here is where the jigsaw pieces start falling into place. We prayed for Canon Lamptey and his lovely wife Evelyn who had just been appointed to lead the work in the Ridge Anglican Church. This is the church that President Nana Akufo-Addo and the First Lady Rebecca attend. Canon Lamptey became the spiritual father to them when he was installed in October 2017 and we were invited to the celebration.

God had been speaking to us about restoring the national altars for the Lord. President Nana made a decision that if the Lord gave him the presidency, one of the first things he would do would be to build an interdenominational national cathedral. He won the election on 7th December 2016 and was sworn in as the 5th President with the help of our friend Chief Justice Georgina Wood on 7th January 2017.

So, true to his word, just minutes before Ghana celebrated sixty years of freedom from British colonial rule on 6th March, President Nana assembled senior church leaders to cut the sod for the foundations of the new cathedral. Another lovely piece of the jigsaw was that President Nana invited our friend Justice Akrofi to cut the sod with him. God was making sure that "justice" is going to break through in Ghana.

We arranged to meet our friend Rebecca who is now the first lady of Ghana. Rebecca is so busy every day with huge queues of people waiting to see her and this day was no different. Despite that, we were really blessed to go straight in. Rebecca and Shirley greeted us warmly and we had a very powerful time with them. It was clear to see that God was certainly blessing them. We were so encouraged to hear that her husband President Nana is working exceptionally hard to see Ghana improve.

We were thrilled to meet Chief Justice Georgina Wood again and be greeted like long lost friends. We had an awesome time together, as she was preparing to retire in a few months.

Missing

Georgina shared a burden she had for a Ghanaian woman called Charlotte Nikoi who was the Associate Director for the UN Children's Fund (UNICEF). Charlotte went missing whilst walking with her husband Chris and their daughter at Table Mountain in South Africa five weeks earlier (when Steve and I were actually in Cape Town). We immediately mobilised everyone to pray and contacted some of our strategic friends in Cape Town to see if they could help.

A friend of ours Greg Kruyer has lots of connections with the police and offered to help. He asked if the Chief Justice could speak to Charlotte's husband, to ask his permission for Greg to speak to the police on his behalf. Once that was approved Greg and Chris (Charlotte's husband) met with the police. The police were quick to tell them that it had been forty days since Charlotte had gone missing and the trail had gone cold.

Greg called me to say that the police had stopped searching and drastic action was needed. He asked if I could speak to Chief Justice Georgina and ask if she could request Ghanaian President Nana to speak to South African President Zuma to help where he could. So, all those calls were made on Friday and by Monday the following news release was made:

8th May 2017 *"President Jacob Zuma has appealed to members of the public who may have information about the missing UNICEF Director Charlotte Nikoi to come forward and assist the police with information. Nikoi is reported to have arrived in Cape Town on 17 March on holiday and to celebrate her wedding anniversary with her family. She went missing on Human Rights Day during a Table Mountain hike. According to the Presidency, Nikoi is a Ghanaian national and is a UNICEF director in New York.*

President Zuma received a special envoy sent by the President of the Republic of Ghana, His Excellency President Nana Akufo-Addo on the sidelines of the World Economic Forum on Africa meeting in Durban, with a special plea for assistance to find Nikoi, said the Presidency.

We appeal to anyone with information to assist the police to locate Ms Nikoi so that she can be reunited with her family. "The South African Police and other departments such as Social Development will continue to provide as much support as possible during this difficult time," said President Zuma."

Five days later Charlotte's body was discovered on the side of Table Mountain where she had collapsed and died from exhaustion. We thanked God that Charlotte's family could now grieve and come to terms with their loss.

The next day was wonderful, as we visited a woman, Paulina Kumah, who was recently bereaved. She has a publishing business, producing and printing a Watchman Newspaper for Christians. She was overwhelmed as we prayed with her and brought some prophetic encouragement. We then drove high up into the mountain area to the Patmos Centre which is a huge prayer centre. An amazing guy called Ebenezer leads this work, and we had a powerful time together as the presence of God was so sweet. We prayed and prophesied over him and a couple of families who were staying there.

As we were leaving, he said we had been sent like angels from the Lord and that he had needed to hear what God had said.

It was late evening by the time we returned to our hotel for a quick change and some food, before going to the Empowerment Worship Centre. We felt like real Africans as we did not arrive until 10pm! The Stewards were directing us to sit on the stage again, but we were pleased as we thought we had managed to slip into some seats at the back without drawing attention to ourselves. We did not see Gideon on the platform, as he was walking about praying and ministering to people. We could not quite see where he was, however, Gideon spotted us and asked in front of 1500 people, "Do you really want to sit there?" We really did! How funny! They really honoured us though and we watched Gideon operate in the most powerful level of the prophetic we have ever seen.

Questions answered

On Saturday we had a dinner appointment with David Ampah-Bennin and his wife Mercy. Chief Justice Georgina had introduced us to them last year and now David is the Commander of the Cape Coast Police. I looked at the photo I took last year, but I still was not sure we would recognise him. So, we asked the Lord to help and they arrived moments later in a huge police vehicle, which was very easy to spot! Thank you, Jesus!

Maria joined us and we had a lovely meal together, chatting and sharing stories of what God is doing as the church connects with the police. David's face was a picture as he carefully listened and became very excited. We talked about the slave trade and explored our hearts to see the issues of sin in the land, reconciliation and healing. We began to plan our next trip and how we could best serve them to see breakthrough come for Cape Coast and Ghana.

We described this trip as an amazing jigsaw puzzle; as we have encountered people it has been as though another piece of the jigsaw has been put into place. Our last Saturday there was one of those days when several pieces went in and we could suddenly see more of the big picture that God was putting together. Thank you, Jesus!

PLANS FOR THE FUTURE

On Sunday, as we were up early, we had plenty of time for the Lord to speak very clearly about the next trip to Ghana. He encouraged us to raise a minimum of £1,000 to be given to the Akrofi Foundation and to be used specifically towards a project for Cape Coast. The project was to be decided by Justice, the bishop of Cape Coast and David the police commander. This would be a one-off gift from Liverpool to help the area of Cape Coast take the first little step towards recovery from the historical impact of the slave trade. The emphasis would be around the people of Cape Coast standing in the gap for their nation, to repent that Ghanaians had snatched, enslaved and sold their own people to the slave traders. You never hear this side of the shocking transatlantic slave trade story, but this was the very humbling journey that God was leading us on. The leaders of Cape Coast were ready to do that and so we had six months to begin the preparations for the Apology. Father God said, "This will be a double blessing – releasing the blessing upon Cape Coast and upon Liverpool".

A final blessing and touch of God's favour happened as we made our way home through the airport. Instead of standing in the long queues, we were made to feel very special and ushered through the Diplomats gate!

Father God had done some awesome things here and we were thrilled to be used by Him. Thank you, Jesus! We give God all the glory.

PRAYER: Heavenly Father I thank you that you see the big picture and that you are willing to entrust me to bring pieces of the jigsaw at the right time to help to complete that picture. I ask that you help me to play my part at the right time, and to the best of my ability. Amen.

SURVIVING DISASTER

GHANA SEPTEMBER 2017

We are very thankful for all those who have gone before us in prayer, chains and tears to lay the foundations for what was about to happen. Our constant prayer is always that God has us in the right place, at the right time, with the right people, doing the right thing for heaven to come to earth. We knew the Lord had many divine appointments ahead of us and things that need to be set in place as the incredible Cape Coast Project began to unfold.

Pam could not travel to Ghana in September 2017, so I was pleased that Ali Rimmer was able to join me. Our flights were delayed due to fog and we were assured they were doing their best to get all of our luggage on the aircraft, however I had a horrible nagging feeling that some of our luggage would be lost in transit. Ali's luggage arrived but mine did not, and KLM insisted I had to return personally to the airport to collect it the following night. This meant that our plans to travel to Cape Coast with the team the following day had to be postponed for another day. My, how God laughs at our plans!!

It is good to know that God is faithful and always on time! We joined Sam, Maria and Justice to travel through the busy streets to Georgina's (retired Chief Justice) gated home. She is still granted high level security, so we were all checked out before they opened the gates. However as soon as they saw Justice in the car we were waved through with huge smiles. It was good to see Georgina looking so well and she was pleased to see us. We chatted, catching up with news, before praying and asking God for specific words to help regarding the critical situations we had discussed. It is so humbling and yet so awesome.

We talked of God's plans for Cape Coast and our friend Sam shared the historical slave journey that he had recently travelled. He had visited the places where slaves were kept, punished and many times killed before they got anywhere near the slave castles of Cape Coast. He said he could almost hear the screams and cries of those who had travelled that journey as they were being dragged away from their wives, children and families. It has had a profound impact on him, and he now has a powerful understanding of what needs to be done.

We talked about God's heart for the redemption and destiny of the people of Cape Coast and I shared Psalm 24 from the Passion Translation of the Bible:

> *"God claims the world as His! Everything and everyone belongs to Him! He's the One who pushed back oceans to let the dry ground appear, planting firm foundations for the earth. Who, then, ascends into the presence of the Lord? And who has the privilege of entering into God's Holy Place? Those who are clean – whose works and ways are pure, whose hearts are true and sealed by the truth, those who never deceive, whose words are sure. They will receive the Lord's blessing and righteousness given by the Saviour-God. They will stand before God, for they seek the pleasure of God's face, the God of Jacob.*

> *So, wake up, you living gateways! Lift up your heads, you ageless doors of destiny! Welcome the King of Glory, for He is about to come through you. You ask, "Who is this Glory-King?" The Lord, armed and ready for battle, the Mighty One, invincible in every way! So, wake up, you living gateways, and rejoice! Fling wide, you ageless doors of destiny! Here He comes; the King of Glory is ready to come in. You ask, "Who is this King of Glory?" He's the Lord of Victory, armed and ready for battle, the Mighty One, the invincible Commander"*

This was so apt for our journey as we sought to deal with the horrific history and release afresh the destiny of these precious people from across the communities of Cape Coast, the nation of Ghana and the continent of Africa. God's desire is to do immeasurably more than we can dream or imagine, and we know this is much bigger than we can yet grasp. We know this is about a community, it is about the historical slave trade and it is about the roots of the modern-day slave trade, which is very much alive and destructive. God will be glorified as this unfolds!

I heard from Matladi, a friend from Brussels, that she was coming to Ghana, not only that, but she was coming to attend the African Forum on Religion and Government (AFReG4) for a conference. Matladi said, "This is to work towards reconciliation and reconstruction, visiting Elmina Castle to ask God's forgiveness for what leaders did in selling their own people to slavery". Would you believe this is exactly what God had also called us to do, so we decided to connect!

We drove through very busy streets, filled with people selling just about everything, but thankfully it was not long before we had made it through the crowds and were driving through very lush green countryside. Almost four hours later we arrived at Cape Coast Police Headquarters where we were welcomed into David's office. He had recently been promoted to Commander and it was great to see him again. We had a wonderful time together and shared the story of our journey with the Lord in seeing Liverpool starting to transform.

David told us about standing up on the hill that looks over Cape Coast and being shocked by what he saw. He began asking God lots of questions about Cape Coast and why it was so devastated. The next day he had met with us in Accra and, as we talked over dinner, we had answered all of his questions without even knowing what they were. Only God can do that!

HORRORS OF THE SLAVE CASTLES

We left the police headquarters and continued our journey to Cape Coast Slave Castle. Ali and I stood on the slave castle walls surrounded by ancient gun cannons where we could see the huge and vicious waves thrashing on to the surrounding rocks.

As we looked out over the Atlantic Ocean, in our spirits we could hear the desperate cries and screams of the young African slaves as they fought for breath, as they drowned in the water, helpless, for no one seemingly had heard their voice.

Moments later, our gracious tour guide led us around the castle retracing the steps of the slaves. At times it was overwhelming and impossible to comprehend how people could be so cruel and evil towards other people. We were led down a steep slippery slope into the dark cells where the men were brutally held. As our eyes became accustomed to the darkness, we began to see rows of sculptured skulls on the floor. All different, expressing the uniqueness of the precious men who been viciously held captive for up to three months in this confined space. No toilets, and only the rainwater spilling in to wash away all of the body waste. We were told that we were standing upon decades of excrement, not a nice thought even though we were only there for a matter of a few minutes. Goodness knows what it must have been like for those terrified and heartbroken men, while they waited for months to be taken through the "Door of No Return".

We continued the tour and were led into the punishment cell which had a huge thick door. We had to stoop down to get in, before walking around a little tight bend to find ourselves in a small space with no light or ventilation. They told us that, even if you tried to shout or scream, the door was so thick that your voice would never be heard outside. Suddenly they banged the door shut and in the petrifying darkness that enveloped us, we soon discovered that our breathing became very shallow. We were closed in there for just a few minutes, but it was easy to see that during those terrible days of the slave trade nobody would ever come out of there alive. You could imagine the slaves gasping "I can't breathe!"

It was especially hard to believe that on the top floor there was a church! The slave merchants and officers would regularly meet there to worship Jesus, whilst slave girls were being raped and abused directly below them. I find it impossible to believe that any of them actually had a relationship with Jesus and easier to believe that it was just a religious exercise. (But, apparently George Whitfield, who so many esteem as a magnificent preacher and evangelist, kept his own slaves). Many of the girls would be routinely abused whilst they waited for the next slave ship to arrive. Some of the women would become pregnant, starting another massive problem, as the children born would be named after the slave merchants. Once pregnant they would not be sold and would not fit back into their local society either.

Once passed as fit and purchased for transit, the slaves would walk past the many slave cells, down the slope and through the huge "Doors of No Return". You could just imagine the horror of these petrified and degraded people, as they were chained and dragged on board the small vessel that would take them to the slave ship and away from their families forever. The dead and the dying would be simply thrown into the violent sea, weighted down to ensure they could not survive.

As we passed through, it was a different story. The sun was shining brightly as we watched men and boys mending their fishing nets alongside their boats, as far as the eye could see. The good news for us was that the "Door of No Return" was open and we were able to return. The male dungeon, the tunnels, the female dungeon, the cell, the "Door of No Return" were all too overbearing to contemplate. How could this have happened? We felt led prophetically to rename the "Door of No Return" as the "Door of Destiny".

There were two good things that came from Cape Coast: the first judicial court in Ghana and the capital city of Ghana. After the slave trade was over, the British established the government capital in Cape Coast which was eventually moved to Accra. Then, sixty years ago, the British withdrew, and the government was back in the hands of the Ghanaians.

We left the physical slave castle behind us but struggled to shake off the impact it had. We drove through the busy streets until all the little businesses had disappeared, and we were bumping along on a dirt track through the countryside once again. It was not long before we were surprised to arrive at a lovely coastal hotel, hidden away in stark contrast to all we had just experienced.

As we alighted from the van, we were shocked to see people with huge machetes greeting us! This was scary, until we realised that they were welcoming us with fresh coconuts and cutting the tops off for us. What a beautiful welcome and the delicious coconut milk was very refreshing.

We had a lovely evening and a good night's sleep with only the pounding of the waves to disturb us. The following day, Saturday, was an early start so we could attend the ordination service of two of the priests at Christ Church Cathedral. Our lovely friend Justice, as retired Archbishop of West Africa, was helping Bishop Victor from Cape Coast with the ordination. The service was beautiful, full of powerful words and declarations. Canon Samuel Lamptey preached an inspiring message to a very full house. The joyful worship was heartfelt, and it was wonderful to see people generously giving, dancing, and singing with gratitude for all that the Lord had done for them. Almost five hours later the service came to an end, and it was difficult to believe that we were literally just across the road from the slave castle we had visited just yesterday.

THE SOUND OF CRUNCHING

We all piled back into the minibus for the journey back to Accra and the journey was uneventful until 5pm, when we encountered heavy chaotic African traffic! What should have been one lane of traffic going in each direction had become *anything goes* – there were at least four lanes of traffic now going in the same direction as us. Vehicles of all shapes and sizes were just doing their own thing, hooting, tooting, and pushing in front without any warning. We did not make much progress and before long it was dark, adding further to the mayhem. There was no control whatsoever and it seemed inevitable that eventually there was going to be a collision.

A car full of men appeared from the right of us and just barged into our space! There was a horrible sound of crunching metal, as their car hit our van. Our driver was very calm and did not even get out of the van to look at the damage. This is Africa after all!! However, the guys in the car were furious because their vehicle had sustained some damages to the left front wing, they did not seem to recognise that they had literally barged into our space!

The traffic was moving at a snail's pace, which meant we could not get away from these guys very easily. A couple of them jumped out of their car and started shouting and screaming at our driver, banging on the windows of our minibus. Our driver just kept looking straight ahead and did not seem to think they should exchange details. Life on the road in Africa certainly improves your prayer life, and Ali and I were praying with great passion as you can imagine. After many hours crawling through the darkness we were relieved to arrive back at our hotel in Accra.

Sunday morning was an early start as it was our friend Canon Samuel Lamptey's first service as minister of the Ridge Church. The service started at 7.30am and we were a little surprised to see the building surrounded by heavily armed soldiers. This was a good indication that President Nana and Rebecca were coming. The worship had started when we heard the police sirens approaching and, moments later, they slipped into their seats at the front without pomp or ceremony and the service continued undisturbed.

The "peace" was fabulous as everyone greeted each other and it was an opportunity for Maria to introduce us again to Rebecca, who then presented me to her husband, the President. I could see God's hand clearly upon him, as later he knelt at the altar rail like everyone else to receive communion. I could see an outpouring of God's love, favour and anointing cascading over his head, as he was down on his knees. I could see that God was going to use him very powerfully, as all that was pouring out upon him would flow out to soak all those in government around him. They are certainly God's people for the leadership of the nation at this time. This is so encouraging for the nation of Ghana as they are poised for massive transformation in the days and years ahead.

Reconciliation and reconstruction

Monday was a truly remarkable day! We arrived back at Cape Coast and then drove on to the Coconut Grove Beach Resort. This was the venue for AFReG4 where we would meet up with our friend Matladi.

AFReG4 describes itself as, "A gathering of Christians involved in government and transformation". People were there from more than 25 African nations and the theme was "Africans Rising Together: Reconciliation and Reconstruction". Just up our street!!! They had not met for four years and they usually meet in different parts of Africa. They just happened to be in Cape Coast for the same days as us! Can you believe that!

This is a quote from their conference literature, "If it pleases the Father to release His mind to us, this gathering could mark a turning point in the history of Christianity on the continent. AFReG4 is about awakening a sleeping giant; it is about releasing the spark that will light fires across the continent as Africa's sons and daughters come together. This could very well be a game changer".

We were ushered in and warmly welcomed from the front. I wondered if I would manage to see Matladi amongst so many precious people. What a privilege to hear so many hearts passionate for their nations and for the whole continent of Africa too. Soon Maria and I were invited to speak for 15 minutes. On hearing my name Matladi turned around – she was actually just a few rows ahead of me with an empty seat next to her. It was amazing to speak there, as clearly God was already moving very powerfully.

Maria shared about how she had arrived in Liverpool and the shock she had felt, seeing it so broken and derelict, rather like Cape Coast that she had left behind. I picked up from where Maria left off and shared how Liverpool had repented about the slave trade; how God had told us He had forgiven us and that now we are called to sow life. Finally, I prayed for everyone, sensing God was about to do something special.

There was a great response and it was wonderful that the Lord had reserved a seat for me right next to Matladi. David, the police commander was given a huge welcome as he arrived a few minutes later and was ushered to sit in the front row. When the break for dinner came, Ali and I had the joy of riding back to our hotel in David's car. It was easy to cut through the dark tiny crowded streets full of people and vehicles. Any hindrances, and the flashing lights and sirens were switched on to clear the way. At one point the road was jammed tight and one of the police officers simply jumped out and took command, clearing the way ahead of us with great speed. Ali and I felt like royalty!

David joined us for a lovely meal at our hotel. We shared stories, encouraged one another, and laughed a lot; full of expectations of what God was about to do.

WASHING BEAUTIFUL FEET

Tuesday morning, we met with several church leaders and Bishop Victor who welcomed us all. He explained how he believed God was in the midst of this. Yes, God is in the midst of this, big style! I shared some of Liverpool's story and then we talked about the issues effecting Cape Coast and spent some time praying together. I felt it was important that we should wash and anoint Bishop Victor's feet to clear away the last season and make way for the new. Ali and I took responsibility for washing Bishop Victor's feet followed by Archbishop Justice's feet. Then the rest of the team all wanted their feet washing and anointing too. It was a very powerful time for us all with lots of tears. This had been an amazing opportunity to see faith grow, as we were all beginning to believe that God could walk through history to bring breakthrough and shift a nation back into its destiny.

Early Wednesday I read Romans 8 from the Passion Translation, which seemed so relevant for us all on this particular day. If you have not read it you need to, as it is so inspiring. We worshipped and prayed, welcoming the Lord to have His way in our midst. After the introductions I shared the story of Liverpool and the journey that the Lord had taken us on to see the start of the transformation. I spoke of Liverpool's repentance and forgiveness, and how that had brought so many breakthroughs. In the second session I spoke about identity and how the orphan spirit can affect us all. Clearly this would be a huge issue in a place like Cape Coast where so many children lost their mothers and fathers. There was a time of discussion and input from everyone present that was very honest and refreshing, as they examined the consequences of the slave trade. These leaders were so precious, as they humbly began to identify the issues which would need to be dealt with through repentance and forgiveness in the days ahead.

There is so much to be done but there is such a sense that these humble people are willing to position themselves, between their history and their future, between heaven and earth, to see God smile upon their land and people once again. They began to identify the role the church had played, is playing, and should be playing, and how they were going to go forward together, led by the Akrofi Foundation.

Ali brought this very powerful word:

A note from Abba Father Daddy to Cape Coast, "I love you My children with an everlasting love. You do not need to earn it. I have already bought it for you through the precious blood of My son Jesus Christ. He took it all for you – all your sins, your shame, your rejection, your guilt, your condemnation, your failures, your sicknesses and He carried it all for you. It is by the blood of My son that you have been rescued, delivered and ransomed from death. For the wages of sin are death but Jesus came to set you free, to give you eternal life, to give you life in all its fullness and abundance.

Do not allow Satan to deceive you, to destroy you, to steal from you, all that Jesus won for you because then My death would have been in vain – worthless. Can you see My precious children I AM VICTORIOUS – I HAVE OVERCOME all spiritual principalities? They have no power (only if you let them have it). I AM GOD. There is no other – there is no one to compare with me.

I can identify with your sufferings, with the pain of the past, the sorrows, and the torture – the betrayal, the rejection, the captivity and the bondage. Can you see that My son Jesus, suffered as you did – the temptations in the wilderness, the constant plots to kill Him behind his back, the subtle and devious ways of trying to outwit Him and outmanoeuvre Him. But I was always going to win! No stripping, lashing of whips, torture could ever thwart my will. Led like a lamb to the slaughter He did not say a word. Drinking the cup of suffering set before Him He was crucified for your sins. Separated from His Father (you'll never know how much this grieved me), He succumbed to My will in order that you could be set free. Risen, ascended He is now glorified in heaven with me, interceding for you.

Can you see my precious children of Cape Coast no matter what you go through, no matter what you have been through I understand? 'Father forgive them for they know not what they do.' They have been blinded by the god of this age.

FORGIVE, my precious children, LET GO! I have dealt with it all through the blood of My precious son. Can you see the LIFE in the blood? Live lives of freedom. Forgive, as I have forgiven you. Love one another, as I have loved you. There is no greater love than a Father laying down His Son's life for the sake of the world. IT IS FINISHED! IT HAS BEEN COMPLETED! Live in the victory secured by My dear son Jesus. Be my glorious people, displaying My glory to the rest of the world. From your Daddy."

Starting to heal the "Middle Passage"

Later we joined the AFReG4 Conference again and had a few minutes before the Reconciliation Service began. Ali and I walked along the beach, watching the waves thrashing on to the sandy shore. We were refreshed by listening to the thundering of the water; the waves came in one after another, as they had done since God created the Gold Coast. It would have been easy to think we were in some beautiful luxurious holiday destination and not a place once consumed with such horror.

The Reconciliation Service started, with everyone gathering around a boat on the grass near to the beach. Some beautiful leaders from Africa and America led the service, ready to complete the journey of repentance and forgiveness that they had been on for some time. The focus was around the "Middle Passage" of the slave trade from Africa to America and the heartbreak of what the Africans had done, or not done to help their own people, as they were enslaved. We were encouraged to follow their lead and allow ourselves to feel the deep pain of this open wound that has existed throughout so many generations. I quickly spotted my friend Matladi and we walked the journey hand in hand.

They began the prayers and led us from the boat to an area very close to the beach. By this point the sky had become very dark and the wind was blowing strongly. We approached a shelter made up of four poles with a thatch covering and we were encouraged to imagine it was the "Door of No Return". We were told to walk through the "Door of No Return" and onto the beach. As we got there it began to rain and the picturesque scene that Ali and I had experienced just half an hour earlier did not look so beautiful now. There were many people passing through the "Door of No Return" but, as we were walking underneath, the leaders suddenly stopped, and we could go no further. Ali, Matladi and I were stuck in the "Door of No Return" and, looking over the shoulders of the leaders, we could see the sea thrashing about violently waiting to see whom it could devour. The clouds were dark and ominous, spewing out rain, whilst many simply stood in shock at what we were visualising. In the distance we could imagine the monstrous slave ship waiting for the broken-hearted slaves to be dragged on board.

Those leading the repentance were standing right in front of us and a lady from America began to explain how the transatlantic slave trade had affected her ancestors. She told of all those who had survived the excruciating journey, whilst tragically some died on the way. She spoke of how many generations had been left bewildered and traumatised by their own people, who had captured and sold them to the traders. One of the Ghanaian chiefs spoke next, a beautiful man dressed all in gold and yellow traditional dress, with a magnificent gold necklace around his neck. He gently began with incredible humility to repent and apologise on behalf of his people, to all those who had come. There were lots and lots of tears . . .

I was overcome emotionally and spiritually. I could not cope with the shame and the guilt of what the people of Liverpool had done. The grief and the pain were unbearable, and I was sobbing. I was grateful for Ali's hand on my shoulder and Matladi's beautiful black African hand gripping my white Liverpool hand reassuringly. I could not verbalise what was happening to me, thankfully I think the Lord had shown them. I wanted to scream out that I was sorry, but I had no voice. I was struggling to breathe – it was as though we were shut up, back inside the cell that we had stood in just a few days ago, where you can scream, but nobody will hear you!

Meanwhile, in front of us another kind-faced American leader had stepped forward to release forgiveness to the Ghanaian chief and his people. Inside I was screaming on behalf of my people of Liverpool, "I'm so sorry, I'm sorry" but nobody except God could hear me.

Moments later, we were told about John Newton and how, as a Liverpool slave merchant, he would have heard the African slaves singing and humming tunes. Of course, one of the most beautiful and popular hymns came from John Newton, "Amazing Grace," after he had encountered God and became a supporter of the Abolitionists. We were asked to hum the tune to Amazing Grace and the sound was so deep and so sweet, but I was so choked up, I could not make a sound.

The Lord suddenly spoke to me, *"Your voice does not need to be heard because I have forgiven you and I have forgiven Liverpool. You are here to sow life and to help others to be healed and reconciled"*. In that one moment God was lifting the heavy yoke of shame and washing me and Liverpool clean. I felt this huge wave of peace fill my heart and it felt like we (Liverpool) had just instantaneously been shifted dramatically into a new place spiritually.

We moved away from the "Door of No Return" with cheering and singing as people were restored, reconciled, healed and changed forever. The next stage involved some powerful declarations and beautiful songs and, as the night drew in, thankfully the rain stopped. Prophetically we lifted the chains off and shouted with one voice that the Africans had returned and were arising. Together in groups of five we held hands and gave thanks to God, praying that the destiny of Africa would be realised, and transformation would soon come.

We walked back to the Conference Centre with Matladi and she told us all that had happened since our visit on Monday evening. You may recall Maria and I had shared the story of Liverpool and the transformation that God was bringing, because we had repented and prayed to see positive change. Matladi told us how people had been very impacted by what we had shared in just a few minutes and how the Holy Spirit had come when we prayed. They watched the video of Lord David Alton and others visiting Benin with the Embrace the Reconciliation Statue and the Declaration of Repentance. You can read more about that in my second book *Extravagant Adventures*. People were shocked and amazed that the Lord had brought us there from Liverpool, at the beginning of the conference to share, encourage and bless them.

It became so clear to us that indeed Liverpool had gone ahead to bring the breakthrough. Breakthrough not just for Liverpool, but also as a gateway place, Liverpool is always going to impact the nations. Now breakthrough is on its way for Cape Coast, Ghana and all of those affected by this ugly business, not just historically but the current slave trade today too.

We said "Goodbye" to Matladi once again and drove away through the dark crowded streets; sadly, this time without a police escort! We were planning to try to have an early night as Archbishop Justice needed to be back to preach at a funeral in Accra by 8.30am, meaning we had to be ready to leave by 3.50am! We had just ordered our meals back at the hotel when we heard sirens and then David arrived. We were thrilled to see him once again and to have an opportunity to encourage him by praying for him and washing his feet.

We finished packing in awe of God and all that He had done through this wonderful little team and the AFReg4 Team. Glory to God who co-ordinated all our diaries so that we could all be there at the same time.

We had a good journey back to Accra and Ali and I had a day of rest in the lovely sunshine by the pool. The Lord provided us with our own little swimming and diving demonstration by a beautiful little kingfisher. I love those treasured moments from the Lord amid the busyness.

RECKLESS LOVE

Friday evening was time for us to visit the Worship Empowerment Centre – what joy! We love the lively vibrant praise and the powerful preaching led by Prophet Gideon, who had just started preaching as we arrived. We were quickly ushered to the seats set aside for guests near to the front. After Gideon had finished the worship continued – everyone singing wholeheartedly, and the room was filled with exuberant praise. We learned a new song written by Cory Asbury called "Reckless Love" which became an anthem for the rest of our trip. This song became very popular and every time we heard or sang it, we had flashbacks of God's saving power through an incident that was about to unfold.

"Before I spoke a word, You were singing over me
You have been so, so good to me
Before I took a breath, You breathed Your life in me
You have been so, so kind to me

Oh, the overwhelming, never-ending, reckless love of God
Oh, it chases me down, fights 'til I'm found,
leaves the ninety-nine, I couldn't earn it, and I don't deserve it,
Still You give Yourself away
Oh, the overwhelming, never-ending, reckless love of God.

When I was Your foe, still Your love fought for me
You have been so, so good to me
When I felt no worth, You paid it all for me
You have been so, so kind to me

There's no shadow You won't light up
Mountain You won't climb up, coming after me

There's no wall You won't kick down
Lie you won't tear down, Coming after me[6]

This song has meant so much to me not just because of what God saved us from. To know that, even as I was being born into a chaotic family, God was singing over me. I was a total mess and yet despite that God chose me. Even when I did not love God, He loved me – not just loved me a little bit, but passionately loved me. I certainly had a long season when I had no self-esteem and felt completely worthless. This was made worse by the spiritual abuse I experienced in one of the churches we attended. However, God was building my character through the time of complete brokenness. (You can read the story in *Extravagant Fire*.)

God certainly kicked down many walls of division and disunity around me, that I could never have dismantled on my own. Most importantly my heavenly Father had exposed many lies that had been told about me and thankfully prompted many of the leaders to repent and apologise. So, this song was so powerful for me, but we had not seen anything yet!

The importance of having the CWM Team behind us back in Liverpool, praying for us cannot be over-emphasised. Each day we are away, we send an email out which says what we have been doing that day and things for prayer for the next day. Today I wrote, "We will be meeting with a friend up in a retreat in the mountains again. Please pray for safe travels there and back". This turned out to be paramount!

Saturday started so well with meetings at our hotel as people came for prayer from 9am. In the afternoon we were collected by our driver, George, and with Maria we began our journey up into the mountains to see Dr Abboah-Offei at his church in Akropong. We were just approaching the mountain when it began to rain very heavily and instantly the roads flooded. We could hardly see the way ahead, so Ali and I quietly prayed in

---

6. Cory Asbury "Reckless Love" from album *Reckless Love* (Redding CA, Bethel Music, 2018)

the back of the car. George was great and just took his time climbing up the steep road ahead.

We drove through the clouds and, thankfully, the rain stopped. At the top we were confronted with very crowded streets, as there was a pagan festival on celebrating one of the many false gods! The traffic was very slow moving when we heard the roaring of engines behind us. Moments later we had three motorbike riders confronting our vehicle, one of them was wearing a horrible ugly mask. They were clearly trying to frighten us as they kept glaring into the car at us and attempting to intimidate our driver. We immediately began to pray again for God's divine protection and that we could get away from these bikers quickly. George remained unflustered and focussed, making his way through the busy streets until we left them behind in the crowds.

We soon found ourselves at a huge lively church and the sound of vibrant worship filled the air. We walked in to witness lots of people totally absorbed in God's presence and giving Him the worship He deserves. We were led to seats at the front where we were greeted by Dr Ebenezer Abboah, who I had met before. We were asked to speak, and we encouraged them by sharing what God had been doing. When the service had drawn to a close, we had a private meeting with Ebenezer. We discussed the Cape Coast project and the desire to see repentance, reconciliation and transformation come for the part that Ghana had played in the transatlantic slave trade.

By the time we left it was 6.30pm and we had no idea what lay ahead of us. It was dark both physically and spiritually, and there was a storm brewing as lightening flashes came in quick succession across the sky. But at least it was dry, enabling us to make good progress through the streets and it was not long before we were making our way down the mountain.

Explosions and panic

On the way David (the police commander) spoke with us on the phone. It was good to chat to him about the time we had together in Cape Coast, the plans for the future, and to pray for him. After an hour travelling, we were starting to feel hungry, as we had not eaten since breakfast. The traffic was flowing well ahead of us and we thought it would not be long before we would be back at our hotel. However, without warning we suddenly saw the whole sky just ahead of us turn a strange shade of orange, before there was suddenly a huge explosion. It looked like an atom bomb had gone off, as a huge fireball rose high into the sky ahead of us, trailing flames everywhere. This was certainly not good news!!!

We continued driving for a few minutes before we were confronted with complete, utter chaos as fear suddenly dominated the whole atmosphere. Cars were crammed together with almost nowhere to go, people were screaming and shouting with looks of absolute terror on their faces. We heard them shouting that there had been a gas explosion and there was a huge fire spreading rapidly towards us.

I quickly called Steve and briefly told him we were ok and asked him to send a message out on Facebook for people to pray. I also sent messages to Rosemary and others to get people praying quickly, not only for us but for all those affected by this unfolding disaster. From the explosion we had seen, we knew that anyone in the immediate vicinity had little hope of surviving.

Clearly, we were not going to be able to continue driving in that direction! Maria rang David and we told him what had just happened. Moments later he called us back to give our driver directions to get us back to our hotel safely. We were so grateful as there was no satnav in the car to guide us. Our driver George was very calm, as he turned the local radio station on which was very informative. They had halted their normal program to give instructions to people out and about near to the fire. They calmly told us that there had been two massive explosions at the Atomic Junction natural gas station and the filling station nearby was also on fire! There was a petrol tanker with a pipe coming out of the back, which was also alight and in very great danger of exploding too! We later heard that the firemen were hosing the tanker down trying to avert further disaster. This was all happening less than ten minutes from our hotel!

George turned the car around, as did many of the drivers in the midst of horns honking and people screaming. The sheer terror and panic on people's faces was dreadful to see. We turned off the road following other vehicles down a dirt track road but realised very quickly that it was not going to be a safe route. Minutes later we were back on the motorway but facing in the wrong direction! Our driver, George sped away in the direction we had just come from, heading back up the mountain again but in the wrong lanes. Thankfully, it seemed all other vehicles coming down had disappeared, as though an angel had supernaturally intervened to make room for people to escape.

A panicking driver in a white van ahead of us mounted the central reservation, and for a few moments rocked back and forth violently as though it was going to topple over. We knew that if it did, the whole road would be blocked including our escape route. Thankfully, as we prayed, it tipped back on to four wheels and drove off on the right side of the road. People were doing crazy things out of sheer fear and panic. Moments later we had changed lanes and at least the threat of vehicles coming directly towards us had ended. A while later we were driving up the mountain once again and from a safe distance, we could see that the huge fire was still blazing strongly.

We had been praying from the moment we witnessed the fireball and looking at the size of the fire, we thought it would be a good idea for us to pray that it would rain heavily. Maria prayed for God to send heavy rain to help put the fire out and immediately it started to rain . . . very heavily. So heavy in fact that it was hard to see the way ahead! At the top of the mountain George suddenly turned to the left and after a few minutes we were bumping along on dirt track roads. The road had already turned into a torrential river, and it was impossible for George to see where the potholes or the bumps were in the road. There was almost no lighting and there were steep drops down the mountainside to one side, so we really had to trust God. We were grateful that Maria had ordered a 4x4 and George was an amazing driver, otherwise we would have been in a lot of trouble.

As we asked God for help again, the sky lit up with forked lightening all around us lighting up the way ahead. We knew that in the natural we were in great danger, but our spirits were at peace knowing that somehow God would get us back down the mountain again safely. We knew that many people were praying for us and for those close to the fireball.

During the journey back to our hotel we could hear the disaster unfolding live on the radio. One woman had been so panic-stricken she had fled from her car leaving her little baby still strapped inside. Cars had been abandoned in the traffic jams and people were running in terror from their homes. Messages were coming in about missing children from anxious and hysterical parents. Throughout it all, Ali, Maria and I sat in the car praying and worshipping God. We were reassured knowing that people were praying back home for us all and God was with us.

Eventually the car arrived at the bottom of the mountain and turned on to a well-lit road once again. The roads this side of Accra were clear, and we proceeded through the heavy rain and flooded streets. We continued praying and then we realised that we had not been specific enough in the prayer for the heavy rain! We suggested that Maria should tell the rain to stop everywhere except for where the fire was. Immediately as she prayed, the rain literally stopped and we drove on, arriving at our hotel just after 10pm, three hours later than expected but safe.

We waved goodbye to Maria and George, and walked into the hotel, shaken but at peace. The first thing we did as we got into our room was thank God for getting us back safely. We were so grateful to everyone who prayed us back to the safety of our hotel – thank you! Then we contacted our families and those praying to let them know we were back at our hotel before we ordered some food in our room. We were both shivering, although the room was warm, and we realised that we were in shock. We spent some time continuing to pray for those affected before we eventually fell asleep.

It is important to note that on a day that was dedicated to the worship of false gods, such devastation and fear was released. The next day we heard that at least seven people had died and over one hundred and thirty-two had been injured but we knew it could have been a lot worse. You may recall seeing it in the UK news as it was actually reported across the world. We continued to pray for all those bereaved, injured and traumatised. We prayed too that the authorities would learn the lessons to ensure this did not happen again. Apparently, this was not the first time and last time over one hundred people had died, and many were injured.

On Sunday morning Ali and I awoke grateful to be alive and thankful to be attending the Worship Empowerment Centre. The church was packed full and we had a wonderful surprise as Felicia (Bishop Festus' wife) had travelled overnight for twelve hours to join us for the day. Once again, the worship was incredible and a special moment for us all was when we powerfully sang, "It is well with my soul". Wow!

Gideon was preaching and brought a powerful and very relevant word about knowing the word of the Lord for your life. He said, "When you are filled with Holy Spirit you should be filled with peace, hope and joy etc. We should have peace no matter what our circumstances may try to dictate". He gave the example of the explosion we had witnessed the previous night and how more people were injured because of their response to the explosion, than because of the explosion itself. Sadly, most of those injured had been hurt during the panic. So many people allow fear to cause chaos and react accordingly when we should bring peace because of God in us. There was a great response and then I was asked to close the meeting in prayer.

We departed for lunch at our hotel and it was good to be together with Felicia again. Bishop Enoch Thompson from the Baptist churches also arrived from a service to join us for lunch. He had heard Maria and I speak at the AFReG4 conference and asked Sam if he could meet up with us. We loved his heart straight away, as he shared about how the Baptist Churches were raising funds and redeeming girls who had been sold or given by their families to the fetish temples. At last I had met someone who had noticed them and was working to release them, not just from modern slavery but also into their destinies. Thank God for them! We prayed for Bishop Enoch and then he prayed for us. What a privilege that was for us!

Justice arrived mid-afternoon followed a few minutes later by Bishop Festus (Felicia's husband). We had a lovely time praying for them and then Bishop Festus prayed for us. Thank You Jesus for such a blessing.

We watched as the time was speeding away from us and finally, we had to leave for the airport. We said our goodbyes and hugged one another, not really wanting to let each other go. Ali and I climbed into the hotel minibus and waved until we could not see them any longer.

It was not long before we were fastening our seat belts and ready for take-off, ready to close the chapter on another exciting adventure with God. Thanking God for the extravagant breakthroughs we had experienced and for all He had done. We were so grateful for all the foundations laid for the next trip and all the beautiful people we had met.

We gave God the glory for all that He has done, is doing and will do as this story unfolds in the days ahead.

PRAYER: Heavenly Father I ask you to forgive me when I take your protection for granted. Thank you for the moments that you have intervened on my behalf to keep me safe. I pray that you will guide me every day so that I am always in the right place, with the right people, doing the right thing, at the right time. Amen.

Grace And Favour

Ghana 2018

I have to be honest and say that if someone had said I did not have to go on this trip in August 2018, I would have been so happy. My mum-in-law was poorly, and I desperately wanted to stay home to support my family, but they knew this was an important trip and urged me to go. Even boarding the flight, I would happily have turned around and gone home but God would not allow me to. However, over the years I have learned that these moments that cost us the most, are often the times of the biggest breakthroughs. They are called extravagant breakthroughs because God empowers us to do what is impossible for us to do in the natural.

We arrived in Accra, slept overnight and then we were on the road to Cape Coast. Since our last trip to Ghana, Justice and Maria Akrofi, Sam and the team had been working very hard in preparation for this time. After settling into our hotel in Cape Coast, we were driven five minutes around to the school where the "Maidens Conference" for girls of every age from the Anglican Diocese was being hosted. It was starting to get dark, but we could just about see our beautiful friend Maria sitting chatting in the courtyard. Around us the dormitories where filling up fast as girls were scurrying about carrying mattresses and bags from the vehicles. We could hear the sound of excited girls, clearly enjoying the opportunity to be away from home.

The next day, after a good night's sleep, we were ushered into the first-floor meeting hall that was full of noisy, excited girls of every age. We were led to our seats next to the headmaster and the Tribal Queen Mother who was chair of the opening ceremony. There was lots of singing in the local language before inspiring speeches from the Queen Mother and the headmaster. Moments later the Queen Mother was introducing me! With no warning, I shared for a few moments and invited the Holy Spirit to come and thankfully He did. We were glad to have an opportunity to pray for the Queen Mother and give her a prophetic word of encouragement.

We had the privilege of praying for two young priests Prince and Maclean who were about to be ordained and allocated their first parishes. God spoke clearly and encouraged them in their journey.

RELEASING THE KEYS

Ali and I went into the Chapel with Mary, one of the intercessors, to create a prayer space for the girls to come and spend time with God. We began to worship, and the presence of God came upon all three of us. Ali and I began to release powerful prophetic declarations over Cape Coast and ended up experiencing God's presence very powerfully ourselves!

Ali and I began to pray for some of the team and to release the keys God had asked us to bring. Steve and I had spent hours at home sorting eight hundred keys and putting tags on them before the CWM Team prayed over them all. We knew that God was going to move powerfully as we distributed the keys and he certainly did. Here are some of the words God gave to us for those who receive the keys:

Revelation 3:7: *"The key of David – What he opens no one can shut, and what he shuts no one can open."*

Isaiah 22:22: *"The key to the house of David; what he opens no one can shut, and what he shuts no one can open."*

"As keys are distributed to women, there will be a flow of the blood of Jesus that will truly set people free to receive Jesus' love. As women are set free in Cape Coast the breakthrough will come to other regions and nations too. When we take hold of the keys to the Kingdom the captives are set free! My freedom brings you freedom!"

"There is a spiritual empowerment to unlock and release multiple breakthroughs, a breaking of the glass ceiling, walls of confinement and chains of historical bondage and a release of power and authority that will break control and manipulation."

Isaiah 9:2: "The people walking in darkness have seen a great light; on those living in the land of deep darkness a light has dawned. You have enlarged the nation and increased their joy; they rejoice before you as people rejoice at the harvest, as warriors rejoice when dividing the plunder. For as in the day of Midian's defeat, you have shattered the yoke that burdens them, the bar across their shoulders, the rod of their oppressor."

We divided up the five hundred girls into groups to co-ordinate their activities throughout the days. After worship, one group was taken across to the Cape Coast Slave Castle. We were sure it would be a tremendous shock for some of them, who would have little or no real understanding of their own horrific history.

FILLED WITH GOD'S LOVE

The rest of the girls stayed in the hall and Maria's friend Paulina Kumah shared the Gospel powerfully. As she spoke the Holy Spirit came heavily and it was not long before every precious girl in the room stood to their feet to give their life to Jesus. Maria followed through, praying for each of the girls to be filled with our wonderful Holy Spirit. Suddenly the presence of God filled the room once again and so many were in tears as they were encountering God's love, maybe for the first time. Tiny tots, teenagers and women all being filled with God's love. It was great to see Prince and Maclean the two priests we had prayed with yesterday, ministering so powerfully alongside the women. What a holy moment! Praise God!

The afternoon session saw a further one hundred and twenty-five plus girls respond to the Gospel. What an amazing day of salvation! Glory to God! We were so exhausted we were in bed by 6.45pm. You can just imagine how tired we were!

Ali and I had a busy day, teaching, praying and prophesying over nearly six hundred children and some adults on Thursday. We handed them their keys as they came into the Chapel, in groups of ten to fifteen, all ages and all levels of understanding. We had to adapt the teaching each time we did it.

What a privilege to pray for Prince, Maclean and Stephen who are about to become priests soon. Today we gave them their keys and taught them about the authority God had for each one of us. My goodness did they grab hold of the teaching and the keys of authority. They said, "We desperately need this in our churches!" Then they proceeded to help us, interpreting where needed, teaching occasionally, and praying over the girls with us. We just thought we had finished when another fifty-five girls arrived for the final session – the largest group of the day.

Praise God today for all those who have been born again, received the Holy Spirit and their keys of authority. Just imagine what God can do if they are all mobilised for God!

We began talking about the Apology that would be made on 8th September 2018. God brought Joseph, an archdeacon, to join the team.

He had been involved in another aspect of the reconciliation work relating to the slave trade and Liverpool from the Anglican perspective. God was joining the dots and completing the picture to bring a significant supernatural breakthrough.

Powerful life changing encounters

Friday night Ali and I had prayed that if there was anything in our lives that was hindering God coming in power, we wanted to deal with it. During the early hours of Saturday morning I woke up struggling to breathe. I have never had asthma, so I knew it was not an asthma attack, but I was desperately struggling. I cried out to God, "Help me I can't breathe". I glanced at my watch and it was 3am! Ali and I had been exhausted when we got into our beds and we had a very busy day ahead of us on Saturday. I did not want to wake Ali, but I was really struggling, "Help me God, I can't breathe".

As I looked around the large bedroom, I could see a vision of my brother and my mum, standing together in our bedroom! They looked at me and could see I was struggling for my breath, they spoke to each other and then they turned around and disappeared.

I was grateful at this point that the Lord woke Ali, and she began to pray. The Lord had told me to cut off the soul-ties with my mum and my brother. There is a very strong bond between my mum and my brother and every time I was around them, I experienced a strong spiritual backlash. My brother was not at all happy that I was a Christian and had been very nasty at times. Many times, my life had been manipulated by my mum from my childhood, when I was forced to take responsibility for the family. I knew that the Lord wanted me to be set free from false responsibility, shame, guilt and so much more.

> *"For freedom Christ has set us free; stand firm therefore, and do not submit again to a yoke of slavery".* Galatians 5:1 (ESV)

In between huge gasps for breath we prayed and as I forgave them both again, God set me free and lifted the heavy yoke that had been over my life for many years.

We were just settling down peacefully when Ali began to struggle for her breath. I quickly asked her what was happening, and she gasped, “I can’t breathe!” The Holy Spirit took her back to when she was about five or six years old, when she was paddling in the waters of the Conwy estuary. Ali nearly drowned when she found herself being dragged underneath the water by the powerful undercurrents. Despite crying for help, her father could not hear her. However, thankfully, her twin sister realised what was happening and loudly screamed for help. Ali’s Dad responded immediately and swiftly managed to rescue his little daughter.

Clearly as a small child, Ali would not have been able to process those feelings of panic and fear she had experienced. Yet there in Cape Coast, as we prayed, in the early hours of the morning, the Lord set her free from the spirit of fear and trauma, which had been locked up inside her since that time.

We are no longer slaves to fear we are children of God! We proclaimed the blood of Jesus over ourselves and knew that what the enemy had planned for evil God turned around for our good!

We were reminded of the moments we had stood on the walls of the castle looking out over the Atlantic Ocean a few days earlier. Our spirits had heard the desperate cries of the slaves all those years ago, when they had been fighting for their breath, as they drowned with nobody hearing their voice. It was as though the Lord was delivering Ali and I, so He could use us to help to bring freedom to Cape Coast.

Knock knock

Ali and I were exhausted and we had just nodded off to sleep again, when we were awoken half an hour later at 6am by a very unusual and early alarm clock. There was a loud tapping on our bedroom window, which was three floors up. When we gently opened the curtain there was an African pied hornbill! Sadly, these are now very rare in Ghana and in fact when we showed the photo to our friends, nobody had ever seen one in the wild before. Apparently, they had been hunted for their horn, so we were very privileged to see one, let alone have him knock on our window to wake us up.

We knew we were in the right place at the right time because we knew how powerfully God had met with us. We were now positioned by God to be used to bring breakthrough for all those attending these meetings.

On Saturday Maria led the program and Ali and I both shared. It all fitted well together. Ali had such anointing upon her as she shared from Jeremiah 29, that if the children prayed for their city and it prospered, they too would prosper. God challenged them to be part of the breakthrough, so that as they are blessed their city will also be blessed.

I shared some of the Liverpool story, prayed and made some powerful declarations of freedom from bondage, using the chains we had brought from Liverpool as a prophetic activation. The children and adults responded really well. I then went on to share the wonderful gospel and a further 200 plus children and adults responded by giving their lives to Jesus.

Wow! Wow! What a day! It was Sunday and our pied hornbill visited us again this morning at 6am, knocking on the window twice. Today we received more than a double blessing – the final service for the "Maidens' Conference" was amazing. The worship was full of life and Ali and I tried to learn some new dance moves, much to the amusement of the children.

Signs of the Shift

Bishop Victor brought the keys that Pam and I had given him just two years ago to show the girls and preached an incredible message. He spoke about

Moses bringing the children of Israel out of Egypt and that they could not go back. He was challenging the girls to no longer look at the past of Cape Coast and the appalling history of the slave trade, but for them to build the new future. It was time for them all to make a new covenant with God. He was excited that they had all been given new keys and many of them were wearing them.

The shift was so incredible that I was in floods of tears as I realised the massive impact of our obedience. When God calls you to do something – please be obedient, as we never know what God will do as a result! I suddenly got a glimpse of what God was doing and already how far things had shifted since Pam and I came with Maria just two years ago. This week was so powerful with over five hundred children and adults giving their lives to Jesus and so many impacted by His love.

Tuesday, 28th August 2018, took us by surprise as we discovered it was the 500th Anniversary since the first transatlantic slave vessel left Cape Coast. God's timing for us being in Cape Coast was incredible and it was a real sign that breakthrough was certainly coming!

> *"There is a time for everything, and a season for every activity under the heavens: a time to be born and a time to die, a time to plant and a time to uproot, a time to kill and a time to heal, a time to tear down and a time to build, a time to weep and a time to laugh, a time to mourn and a time to dance, a time to scatter stones and a time to gather them, a time to embrace and a time to refrain from embracing, a time to search and a time to give up, a time to keep and a time to throw away, a time to tear and a time to mend, a time to be silent and a time to speak, a time to love and a time to hate, a time for war and a time for peace."* Ecclesiastes 3:1-8

This amazing day started with a visit from our pied hornbill once again. We had missed him as he had not been for a couple of days. However, on Wednesday morning I was awake when I heard a gentle knocking on the window, and I knew straight away that he was visiting us again. I gently woke Ali and we carefully pulled the curtain slightly so we could watch what was happening. Our eyes were fixed on him as he preened himself and then knocked on the window again. We got a shock when, all of a sudden, a second bird flew at the window directly in front of us! This time Mr Hornbill had brought his partner. We decided to call them Grace and Favour.

Grace and Favour were very energetic as they both took turns to fly at the windows and knock rowdily. We lost count of how many times they knocked, but Grace then began to knock persistently and vigorously on the door so loudly. They were determined to wake up any sleepers, in fact it was a wonder they did not wake the whole hotel up!

What did this all mean? As we prayed about it, God gave us lots of revelation. He is arousing the Church.

> *"Ask, and the gift is yours. Seek, and you'll discover. Knock, and the door will be opened for you. For every persistent one will get what he asks for. Every persistent seeker will discover what he longs for. And everyone who knocks persistently will one day find an open door."*
> Matthew 7:7-8 (TPT)

But why the pied hornbills? Apparently, the female pied hornbill can lay up to four white eggs in a tree hole, which is blocked off during incubation with a cement made of mud, droppings and fruit pulp. There is only one narrow aperture, just big enough for the male to transfer food to the mother and their chicks. Whilst they are locked into the nest, it becomes for her, a place of confinement and restraint.

We sensed that Grace, our female hornbill, had not come with her mate Favour as she had been locked up inside the nest. However, on the third day of their trips to us, she was set free and was able to join Favour in visiting us. It was on the third day that Jesus rose from the dead and every day because of that we can break free and be filled with resurrection power.

As the pied hornbill chicks grow, the space in the tree becomes too small for them and the female breaks out. God was saying to us that for too long the girls and women have been confined. Prophetically we knew it was God saying, *"Jesus is breaking them free and smashing the glass ceiling once and for all. It is time for the women to break free and to feed themselves with God's word. To receive an impartation that will awaken them into their destinies instead of being simply confined to just look after their babies. God is releasing women all across the world and this is a time for men and women to begin to minister together. There is a 'commissioning' taking place, signalling the move of God to come and the harvest that will be born out of it".*

We knew God was speaking to us and as we prayed for the day, He touched us very powerfully, preparing us for the second morning of the Women's Conference. Ali taught wonderfully using Esther 1. Together we shared testimonies and the Gospel before celebrating with great joy as we saw a further thirty precious women giving their lives to Jesus.

We returned to our hotel for lunch to find it was busy with a conference bringing the police, council and other agencies together. Over lunch we chatted with two police officers and Ali told them we were from Liverpool. Within minutes we had a divine appointment with the new Chief of Cape Coast Police, Paul Awini, who was excited to meet us. He told us his family lived in Liverpool and his children went to Frontline Church! God is doing exceedingly more than we could dream or imagine.

In the evening, Ali and I ministered from the story of Esther. I shared some of my testimony and spoke about how we needed to break free from the chains of our past in order to step into our destinies. It was a very powerful time particularly for these women as so many of their lives had been overshadowed by the slave trade. Later, as we left, the women took hold of the chains and began to pray for themselves. We later heard they were there for hours until they had received their breakthroughs. Praise God for their freedom.

With impeccable punctuality, Grace and Favour, our two feathered friends visited, 6am Thursday morning on the dot! Amazing! They displayed an ease and familiarity with us as they casually preened themselves. We waited with anticipation to see what the Lord would do today! Before the ladies arrived, Ali and I enjoyed worshipping in the chapel. I began to pray, welcoming the Holy Spirit and releasing revival.

HEAVY PRESENCE OF GOD

We continued teaching and Ali called the women to repentance and forgiveness to deal with the orphan spirit and anything else coming from that. I followed on from Ali speaking about Esther being a woman of grace and favour (remember the names of our African pied hornbills). As I began, suddenly the presence of God began to fall in the room very powerfully. There was a sudden commotion, and someone screamed as she witnessed a woman close to her suddenly passing out. I sensed it was simply Satan wanting to distract us all, so I was determined that we should stay focussed on worshipping Jesus. Maria took the woman to hospital, although we anticipated she would make a full recovery. She was later discharged, as the hospital could find nothing wrong with her as we had expected. When the Holy Spirit comes in power you can often have the demonic in someone start to manifest and so it is important to discern what is happening.

I continued to share, and the presence of God just got stronger and stronger. Everyone present was massively encouraged, as I shared the very powerful testimonies. They loved the story of the multiplication of money in Uganda, and the subsequent money given to pay towards the national debt in Britain that again God multiplied. You need to read this in *Extravagant Adventures* – it is an amazing story. Pastor Spaine was so inspired, he stepped out in faith to challenge everyone to sow money into Cape Coast. People soon responded to the offering and there was a definite shift and breakthrough in the atmosphere. One of the priests called everyone around the altar to pray and the fire of God just got stronger and stronger. It was amazing to witness those young priests so full of fire!

I took a photo that showed the start of a glory cloud, a real sign of God's presence which appeared and moved across from one side of the altar to the other. There was also a breeze that came right through from the back of the church. The windows and side door were open but the breeze we experienced came from a completely different direction. Only God could do that!

I shared the prophetic word about God bringing the glass ceiling down and breaking the walls of confinement. We prophesied that it was a new day and that Jesus was leading His sheep out as in John 10:3-4 *"The gatekeeper opens the gate for Him, and the sheep listen to his voice. He calls his own sheep by name and leads them out. When He has brought out all His own, He goes on ahead of them, and His sheep follow Him because they know His voice".* We preached about Peter before we had another very powerful time with the Holy Spirit, and we sensed that many of these women had really encountered God in a new and dynamic way.

Friday morning Ali wrote: "We were awakened to unbelievable news about the roof collapsing in an ancient church called San Giuseppe Dei Falegnami, located in Central Rome. What was even more interesting and amazing was that this church was built above an ancient prison. The Catholic Church believe that Peter was supposed to have spent his last few hours there in a dungeon before he was hung."[7]

Ali continued, "we were astounded and in total awe. God had revealed through Sue just a few hours earlier, that He is breaking the glass ceiling over women especially but also men. As Peter was the founder of the church, it was as if God was saying so clearly, "It's time for my Church to be freed and loosed from all constraints and limitations that have stopped them from reaching their destinies. It's time for the church to arise in this new season and be all that it was created to be". This is now

---

7. http://news.sky.com/story/roof-of-historic-rome-church-san-giuseppe-dei-falegnam-collaps-es-11486043

the third time in which a physical collapse of a ceiling has been seen after Sue has preached on glass ceilings coming down and John 10."

Drunken driver

Maria was due to meet Bishop Victor, but it had to be postponed as she had to take the woman who collapsed to the hospital. When we joined the rest of the team for breakfast, we heard the news that Maria did not get to meet Bishop Victor until 11pm. So, it was very late when Emmanuel (our driver) dropped Maria back off to our hotel after the meeting. Emmanuel was on his way back to his accommodation when a car collided right into our minibus. It turned out that the driver of the car was drunk and uninsured! The police got involved and called some of our Ghanaian team to help Emmanuel, who thankfully was not injured.

After we had finished breakfast, we discovered the three men including the drunken driver from last night, waiting in reception to meet with us all. The police had given them an opportunity to settle the matter with us, without it going to court. This would definitely not happen in the UK! I told them they would have ended up in prison in the UK, as they could have killed someone or died themselves. I said our driver was called Emmanuel, which means "God with us" and that God had been with him last night and preserved his life and theirs. The driver then told me his name was also Emmanuel! They were all very sorry and the driver was so broken-hearted about what he had done. I told them all they needed to give their lives to Jesus and the next moment they were all on the knees, giving their lives to Him. We prayed with them, asking God to fill them with His Holy Spirit and He did.

As a result of the accident, one of the sliding doors on our minibus was damaged and would not open. It was decided that a mechanic was needed to check that the minibus was safe for us all to travel in. The mechanic quoted a price to fix the minibus and the men who had caused the accident paid up joyfully, without question. Later we heard that the mechanic also gave his life to Jesus. Praise God that He turned something the enemy planned for evil into something so good. Another four souls encountering Jesus . . . yeah God!

LIVES CHANGED FOREVER

Today was the Clergy Wives' Conference and although there were only twelve women, they sat scattered across the chapel and isolated from one another. Maria spoke powerfully with great humour, vulnerability and truth about the issues that clergy wives face. She explained how they need to protect their husbands through prayer and raise themselves to their full potential as they serve alongside them.

After a beautiful communion service led ably by our four enthusiastic and fiery priests, I gave a powerful prophetic word to the ladies. *"There is a dramatic shift of season here and God is breaking the glass ceilings that have restrained and limited you. God is releasing you from the chains and wounds that have restricted you, causing you to miss your destinies because you have withdrawn yourselves. There is a momentum coming and God is asking you to forgive. To open your hearts afresh because He's ready to propel you and release you again into the fullness of what He has created you for. There is a fresh flow of grace, favour and provision coming to you, if you will reposition your heart. This is a time for worship, the great commission and preparation of the Bride".*

We then all gathered close to the altar in a circle, shoulder to shoulder, where we had another incredible time of ministry. I felt led to honour Maria in front of everyone as they had no idea of the incredibly difficult job and long hours she worked in the NHS within the UK. We honoured her for her sacrificial life, offering everything to the work of the Lord. Lots of people prayed for her and we sensed something had dramatically shifted in the heavenlies.

After giving keys to the ladies we began to minister individually, anointing people and speaking prophetic words into their lives. The Holy Spirit moved very powerfully, touching hearts, and we witnessed dramatic breakthroughs as their faces changed before our eyes. The fire of God had fallen once more and where there had been isolation earlier in the day, now there was such a sense of unity and love in the room. We gave God the glory for yet another incredible day of watching the Holy Spirit in action shifting and reshaping Cape Coast.

The next day we travelled back to Accra without event. Praise God! We were thankful to be settled back into the Fiesta Royale Hotel where we enjoyed a meal that was not rice or spring rolls, our diet for the last twelve days!

Sunday was an interesting and mostly enjoyable day. We attended the Worship Empowerment Centre in Accra which we love. We entered the building from the bright sunshine, towards the end of the first service and early for the second. We were quickly ushered down a dark aisle to some seats, but the problem was that the stairs were not lit and despite my best efforts, my eyes could not adjust in time and I could not see where I was going. I have had five operations on my eyes, and my sight is amazing except when I go from the bright light into the dark! I fell heavily, scraping my knees, jarring my wrist and damaging my pride very badly!

However, I quickly forgot about my tumble once the worship began and my focus was back on Jesus again. It is so good to receive when you are giving out so much and they had a great speaker visiting from New York. What a real blessing!

Monday we spent the morning with God and felt more relaxed, rested and refreshed. Praise God! We had a visit early afternoon from the beautiful

Evelyn Hutchful who had lived in Liverpool for a while. Just as soon as Evelyn had gone, a guy came running over to chat to us after he had seen us praying with Evelyn. We found out he was a Muslim who had noticed that we were Christians and asked us to pray for him. It was not too long before we were leading him to Jesus and praying for him to be filled with the Holy Spirit. God has so many divine appointments for us when we make ourselves available whether we are in Ghana, Liverpool or wherever we are. Ali and I could not stop thanking God for all He had done, was doing and would do in our final days here.

Wednesday, we made our final visit to the Worship Empowerment Centre for the 11.30am service. I was invited to speak and spoke on *"Bringing the glass ceiling down"*, Isaiah 61 and declaring, "It's time to step out of the chains". I quoted this fantastic passage from Romans 8:18-21 (TPT) *"I am convinced that any suffering we endure is less than nothing compared to the magnitude of glory that is about to be unveiled within us. The entire universe is standing on tiptoe, yearning to see the unveiling of God's glorious sons and daughters! For against its will the universe itself has had to endure the empty futility resulting from the consequences of human sin. But now, with eager expectation, all creation longs for freedom from its slavery to decay and to experience with us the wonderful freedom coming to God's children."* God is looking to unveil a magnitude of His glory in us! Wow! Are you ready to receive yours?

GRACE IS IN THE AIR

We returned to our hotel only to collect our luggage and then we were all back in the van on our way back to Cape Coast once again. We were very pleased to have Justice with us and we had lots of fun and laughter in the minibus during the three-hour trip. As we arrived on the outskirts of Cape Coast, we saw a boat with the name *"Adom wa wim"* which meant *"Grace is in the air"*. A great sign to us indeed!

Rev. Kofi Johnson arrived to pray with us on Thursday morning to finalise the plans for The Apology as he was hosting and leading it. We were all thrilled at the progress made towards the program for The Apology. People across the churches had been overwhelmed by the speed at which everything was happening and amazed at the number of churches that had come on board. Nobody had expected God to move so quickly and we were thankful for Maria and Justice who were so finely tuned in to hear God's timing.

There were a lot of timely things happening in Ghana – Kofi Annan died on 18th August 2018. Kofi Annan was not just a Ghanaian diplomat but he rose to be the United Nations Secretary General. He was considered to be one of Africa's most illustrious sons and someone who dedicated his life to pursuing peace. Many high-profile international leaders were coming from across the world to attend his funeral on 13th September. Our precious friend Justice was invited to speak at his funeral, and we were also invited to attend. However, we would be back in Liverpool by then, so we sent our apologies via Justice. We knew that God would continue to pour His love, His Spirit and His anointing out through Justice as he ministers there.

As we recalled, 28th August was the 500th anniversary since the first vessels sailed from the Gold Coast full of slaves on the transatlantic trade triangle. We believed it was now time for breakthrough! We honour and recognise so many people and teams who have prayed here in the past. We give thanks to God for all He has done but we know the best is yet to come! Saturday (the day of the Apology) is the final day of the Jewish year 5778 and Rosh Hashanah the start of the new year 5779 is on Sunday. God's timing is indeed perfect!

In the afternoon, Ali and I visited Elmina Castle with Pastor Spaine from Guinea and Veronica from Accra. I had been before with Pam and Maria during our first trip two years ago. For me, the first visit was so shocking, and I felt so much utter hopelessness. The town of Elmina is massively crowded with people everywhere, thousands of fishermen either out fishing or mending and cleaning their nets. People flocked around us trying to sell us trinkets we did not want and the weight of guilt and shame for us as white people was so heavy.

Veronica struggled and who could blame her! These were her people – women who had been stripped and paraded before the soldiers before they chose which ones they would rape. This like all Slave Castles was a brutal place of sexual immorality, degradation, violence, heartbreak, bondage, sickness and of course death.

Ali was shocked as Pam and I had been. The Elmina Castle was so much worse than Cape Coast Castle! It is so hard to comprehend the evil that man could inflict on fellow man. The sin and wickedness committed those hundreds of years still pervades the air and you struggle to breathe as you try to absorb all the atrocities committed.

HOPE ARISING

This time for me felt very different as we stood poised for The Apology on Saturday. I felt such hope starting to arise as I knew God could shift the spiritual atmosphere and bring so many breakthroughs, as we joined with the people of Cape Coast to all humble ourselves before God and each other. There was so much for us all to repent of, but God is a good and merciful Father, who had been waiting to lift the curse from this land and to release His blessing.

The church had been located above the prison cells. How could the church worship, praising God when down below men and women were being chained and imprisoned against their will? Chained in dark, cramped and stinky dungeons, they awaited the arrival of the terrifying slave boats, to take them away from their families and loved ones to an unknown destination. Those who resisted were thrown in the Condemnation Cell, where there was no ventilation and no food – the place where they would suffocate and die. They were the 'Freedom Fighters' as our guide commented.

Yet despite all of this as we walked and travelled the pathway towards the "Door of No Return" we sensed, in this hour there was hope. God was doing a new thing – He is the Great Redeemer – only He can forgive the sins of our ancestors and bring about healing and restoration of the land. As the cries of all those mercilessly thrown from the boats, still call out from the sea, only God could avenge their blood! We knew we were standing at a pivotal time of history – as the Church stood together in unity, with one voice to repent to their own brothers and sisters and to God Almighty. This was the time for God to hear and to heal the land. A sombre but momentous time in His Story.

Ali and I spent the rest of the day helping Justice and Maria draft The Apology, as well as writing the statement from Liverpool and praying.

When we had been praying over the keys we brought out to Ghana, one of our CWM Team had a prophetic word from God about padlocks or lovelocks which have been appearing near to rivers and seas. The lovelock symbolises the love of two people who are committing their hearts to one another, they write their names on the padlock and then lock it on to a bridge or railings. Then they throw the key into the river or sea to demonstrate they can never be pulled apart again.

We knew there were millions of people who loved and were committed to one another, but they had been torn apart by this barbaric slave trade. We felt God wanted us to throw a padlock into the sea as a prophetic act to release all those broken hearts. So we wrote that into the program for The Apology as a prophetic act to break the trauma off all those generations separated by the slave trade.

On Friday, Ali and I did not go out of the hotel as we were really busy preparing the documents for Saturday's Apology in the Cape Coast

Cathedral. We worked with Maria and the rest of the team to finish the actual Apology which is incredibly powerful and moving. I was constantly in tears as we helped to write it and as we read it all through. I did not know how I would get through the day with the weight of it all on my heart.

PRAYER: Heavenly Father I thank you that no matter what has happened in my life your love and power can redeem it and use my life for your glory. I commit my life afresh to you and give you permission to cleanse and heal me. Amen.

The Apology Day

8th September 2018

I awoke at 3.30am with such an excitement in my spirit as I lay in my bed praying for a powerful move of God in Cape Coast. Suddenly I saw a chink of light in the top right-hand corner of the darkened room. As I followed the ray of light down across the room, I prophetically saw before my eyes dry bones scattered across the floor; the bones of all of those scattered so many centuries ago.

God brought me full circle to an incredible vision He had given me many years before. In the vision I saw a similar darkened room with a chink of light coming from a corner of the ceiling. As I looked around the room there were many bones scattered across the floor. These were the bones of the church, scattered and broken as in Ezekiel 37:1-10 (NKJV):

> *"The hand of the Lord came upon me and brought me out in the Spirit of the Lord, and set me down in the midst of the valley; and it was full of bones. Then He caused me to pass by them all around, and behold, there were very many in the open valley; and indeed they were very dry. And He said to me, "Son of man, can these bones live?" So I answered, "O Lord God, You know".*

Again He said to me, "Prophesy to these bones, and say to them, O dry bones, hear the word of the Lord! Thus says the Lord God to these bones: "Surely I will cause breath to enter into you, and you shall live. I will put sinews on you and bring flesh upon you, cover you with skin and put breath in you; and you shall live. Then you shall know that I am the Lord.'"

So I prophesied as I was commanded; and as I prophesied, there was a noise, and suddenly a rattling; and the bones came together, bone to bone. Indeed, as I looked, the sinews and the flesh came upon them, and the skin covered them over; but there was no breath in them.

Also He said to me, "Prophesy to the breath, prophesy, son of man, and say to the breath, 'Thus says the Lord God: "Come from the four winds, O breath, and breathe on these slain, that they may live.'" So I prophesied as He commanded me, and breath came into them, and they lived, and stood upon their feet, an exceedingly great army."

In my vision all those years ago the Lord filled me with His authority. He had me walk through the scattered bones commanding them to arise, to be connected. In the natural I would never want to walk through a dark place filled with the scattered bones of people, but this was different, and God was with me. God is reconciling His people and preparing His Bride ready for when Jesus returns. Wow! Little did we know when we came with Maria to Cape Coast two years ago, what we would all be about to witness.

It was 4.30am and the birds were singing louder than ever trumpeting the dawn of a new day. It was as though they could see and hear the bones shifting, coming together, and rising to release a new beginning across Cape Coast, Ghana, Africa and across the world. It sounded as though they had a new vibrant song to sing over Cape Coast about the new era that was being birthed from this special day: an era of freedom, identity and destiny.

I listened and watched intently not wanting to miss a precious moment of this incredible day. As I drew the curtains back the sky was full of dark clouds. They were pouring out heavy rain, as though all of the tears that had been bottled up for over five hundred years were being released in a huge deluge to wash the land with forgiveness; forgiveness from those whose lives were taken and those whose hearts were broken.

We did not see our African pied hornbill friends Grace and Favour this morning. However, we sensed they had completed their task, releasing the wake-up call. They had knocked and kept knocking with such perseverance until the church here in Cape Coast had woken to the breakthrough of grace and favour to shift and change into the new season.

It had stopped raining by the time we were passing by the coast, but the water was turbulent and was tossing the fishing boats around like they weighed nothing at all. We turned the bend with Cape Coast Slave Castle on our left and arrived at the cathedral opposite. There was such a sense of expectancy as we walked into the cathedral. Many of the clergy had already assembled and were busy robing up or quietly praying in the pews. The worship was sweet and there was such a strong sense of God's presence filling the place.

There were cameras and microphones everywhere as the local TV and radio stations were recording the whole service. The program was full and was expected to last for three hours, starting at 10am and finishing at 1pm.

The interesting thing was that this gathering was today of all days, you see the 1st September was a day of celebrating a huge pagan festival in Cape Coast. The church holds no funerals for two weeks after this festival and if this had been a normal Saturday, it would have been almost impossible to have any church leaders present. Saturday is the day for funerals and often the priests would be holding several funerals one after another. So, once again, we recognised that God had orchestrated this day in a very special way.

THE SERVICE

The Service of Public Apology and Repentance for the Transatlantic Slave Trade by the Ecumenical Community of Cape Coast program was full, emotional, and powerful. We sang a song called "Together" which really broke the ice as everyone danced around the church, hugging one another and sharing "the peace". A wonderful start to the day, when there were so many denominations coming together as one.

Rev. Canon Kofi deGraft-Johnson (Anglican Church) welcomed everyone and set out the purpose of the day. Kofi did an amazing job of hosting this gathering. He was the right man for the job, as he had a slave trading history himself and was passionate about seeing breakthrough come for Cape Coast. He described emotionally some of the journey he was on personally, as he had discovered that his own family lineage was part of the slave trade. Kofi was a direct descendant of both the people of Cape Coast and the slave merchants, as one of the women in his family line had birthed a child fathered by a slave merchant with the surname Johnson. Kofi understood the pain and trauma of the situation only too well. He clearly described the journey we had all been on over the last the last two years.

Kofi welcomed us all and prayed that God would come in response to our prayers to heal the land, so that the next generation could live in peace and enjoy the goodness of the land. He reminded us that because of Jesus' righteousness we could stand to confess our sins.

Maria shared the whole story of our journey together and how David had asked, "Why has Cape Coast deteriorated so much?" Maria even demonstrated the "Something has broken in Cape Coast" dance, which had everyone laughing. When we had been in Accra on a previous trip Maria had woken up in the middle of the night. As she had begun to pray, she suddenly began to dance and sing *"Something has broken in Cape Coast"* over and over and over again. Maria eventually climbed back into bed but was still not able to settle so she got out of bed and began singing and dancing again, "Something has broken in Cape Coast". As she was dancing around their bedroom singing, Justice was awoken, and he climbed out of bed as he recognised God was in this and he did not want to be left out. Can you imagine Justice and Maria dancing around their bedroom singing in the middle of the night? But that was a prophetic song and dance that no doubt released the breakthrough.

Maria spoke of her experience of moving to Liverpool so many years ago and it looking as broken as Cape Coast. God had shown her that every place involved with the slave trade historically, had been broken and it was only repentance and reconciliation that would bring cleansing and healing. Maria had witnessed Liverpool rising from the brokenness and dereliction and asked, "God why?" Later we met and were able to share the journey of prayer and repentance the people of Liverpool had been on for many years.

The priest from the Catholic Church then gave a brief history and overview of how the church had participated in the slave trade. He explained many of the Bible verses relating to slavery and how they had been misunderstood. He mentioned that blood was mentioned 549 times in the Bible and when it was shed unrighteously this was not good and needed to be repented of. He talked of the sin of commission and the sin of omission and how the church had been guilty of that and often still is. The church could have acted but chose not to and even when there was a loud outcry for the abolition of slavery, most of the church stood against it.

The Methodist Church minister then spoke. *"Imagine the pain and sorrow on the hearts of people when the fathers, the breadwinners were separated from their families never to return? Imagine the pain when the mothers were separated from children never to be reconciled? Imagine the pain, the bitterness when the son was taken away, the hope for the family? Imagine the pain when they were put in chains in smelly dungeons to await the day when they would be taken in the slave ships to unfamiliar lands? Some would not even make it. Imagine the pain when humans were naked and auctioned and sold like animals? Imagine our fathers being taken to farmlands where they were paid very little? Imagine the tears shed and the curses left on the land?*

So, we pray and ask forgiveness. We ask for forgiveness because God is so merciful and when we truly repent, he will forgive us. Hear our prayer today and heal, nourish, and replenish our land and environment. May God visit his people again."

The Pentecostal Council declared, *"We are standing with one accord with everyone and with those from Liverpool, to ask God to release forgiveness and to cause His Spirit to descend upon the land again. We can only look to God to help us".*

Osabarimba Kwesi Atta II of the Oguaa Traditional Council (Tribal Chief and King of the Fanti People) shared how he had asked the question, *"Why was Cape Coast not progressing?"* He said he had gone down to the dungeons with ten priests twenty-five years ago to pray and nothing had happened, but perhaps now this was the time for God to be merciful. He declared enough is enough!

He told us that the chiefs never die as their name continues, so, in effect, as his ancestors had been involved, that meant he was guilty too. So, on behalf of himself and the rest of the chiefs he apologised profusely for the consequences of their actions. He wanted to build a positive connection between Liverpool and Cape Coast to build a better future for the children.

There was a statement from someone representing the African American Community. This lady returned from America thirty-one years ago, after being invited back home to Ghana with sixteen other people. Sadly, she was consumed with bitterness and anger, declaring that saying sorry was not enough and there needed to be compensation and recompense for the horrific way her ancestors had been treated. They needed to be paid back for everything they had lost, with homes rebuilt and finances restored.

LIVERPOOL'S STORY

I shared a testimony from Liverpool. In 1999 I asked God why we were not seeing people coming to salvation in Liverpool. He told me that there was a spirit of death over our region because of Liverpool's involvement in the slave trade. As you know, Liverpool had played an active part in the transportation and trading of 1.5 million Africans. This evil trade resulted in the bloodshed and death of many Africans, as well as families being torn apart and sold – some into very bad situations.

For many years since then Christians in Liverpool had cried out to God in sorrow and repentance for what happened during the slave trade years. Our team, Community Watchmen Ministries came in at the end of that season, thanking God for all those who had also prayed, including John Manwell who was there that day. (John Manwell, Christopher Gibaud, Marcus Jeremy and Papa Fasanya had just arrived a few minutes before I was about to get up to speak. They had come to Ghana representing the North West Christian Business Forum looking to connect with local businesses.)

We continued to pray, until a powerful turning point came for Liverpool on 9th December 1999. As a final act of the Millennium, Liverpool City Council unanimously passed a motion apologising for the city's role in the slave trade, linked to a commitment to policies that would end racism and work to create a community where all were equally valued:

"Liverpool City Council expresses its shame and remorse for the City's role in this trade in human misery. The City Council makes an unreserved apology for Liverpool's involvement in the slave trade and its continued effects on the City's Black Communities. The City Council hereby commits

itself to work closely with all Liverpool's communities and partners and with the peoples of those countries which have carried the burden of the slave trade."

During the summer of 2005, the Lord spoke to Community Watchmen Ministries. He said, "Liverpool no longer needs to repent of her past regarding the slave trade. Liverpool is now walking in the forgiveness and blessing of God; however, we now need to sow life into Africa".

Since then, our team worked hard with many partners in Uganda, South Africa, Rwanda and Ghana. We were honoured to work with thousands of church and secular leaders across these African nations.

After the repentance declaration from Liverpool, we began to see the curse that we believe came from our involvement in slavery, lifting from the land, and the blessing of God starting to be released very powerfully.

One of my favourite passages of scripture is Isaiah 61:1-4:

> *"The Spirit of the Sovereign Lord is upon me, because the Lord has anointed me to proclaim good news to the poor. He has sent me to bind up the broken hearted, to proclaim freedom for the captives and release from darkness for the prisoners, to proclaim the year of the Lord's favour and the day of vengeance of our God, to comfort all who mourn, and provide for those who grieve in Zion – to bestow on them a crown of beauty instead of ashes, the oil of joy instead of mourning, and a garment of praise instead of a spirit of despair.*
>
> *They will be called oaks of righteousness, a planting of the Lord for the display of his splendour. They will rebuild the ancient ruins and restore the places long devastated; they will renew the ruined cities that have been devastated for generations."*

For everything negative, we prayed for the positive and have now seen many amazing breakthroughs:

a) When jobs were lost — for every job lost, we prayed for ten new ones. Two years ago, Liverpool was recognised as the place with the largest proportion of fast-growing firms than anywhere else in the UK.

b) Our schools were in very poor state, so we prayed for new schools. We then had the biggest school building program in the whole of Europe.

c) Our River Mersey was very polluted with little life in it. As we prayed, we put salt into the river as Elisha did and over time it became clean. Now it is the cleanest it has been in over one hundred years, with fish and wildlife we had never had before.

d) We have a new and thriving film industry.

e) We have many Muslims becoming Christians.

f) We had very poor housing; now many houses in those areas have been demolished and thousands of beautiful new homes with gardens have been built.

g) Our police were struggling with huge crime issues because of drug gangs. As we prayed, in 2004 Merseyside Police had huge success in drug related crime impacting businesses, bringing hope and seeing many gang members either getting saved or being sent to prison. Police officers were giving their lives to Jesus because of what they saw God doing. We were awarded Citizen of the Year for helping reduce crime . . . all through prayer!

h) We now have a thriving tourist industry and are now the fifth most popular tourist destination in the UK. We have seen the number of hotels more than double in the last ten years and Liverpool welcomed fifty-seven cruise ships in 2018; that is more than 100,000 tourists and that brings more jobs!

i) July 2018, the BBC news came to Liverpool to report on the story of transformation and Liverpool University have employed someone to study the journey as it progresses.

j) A cynical City was won over because people changed! There was a leap of faith and people stopped saying negative things cursing themselves and the city. Instead they began to speak blessings and releasing the destiny of our beloved Liverpool.

k) Liverpool's economic model of transformation has been recognised by the government with the launch of the UK City of Culture.

Mayor of Liverpool, Joe Anderson recently said, "Culture, tourism and visitor economy is now worth £6 billion to our economy. It employs people, creates jobs, opportunities and business growth".

This has not all happened overnight. It has been a process and there have been some disappointments along the way. God has challenged us to be obedient to do the things He has called us to. We have prayed fervently and consistently. We have not given up in believing that God desires to do immeasurably more than we can dream or imagine. We began to dream big dreams for our city, and we are beginning to understand that God wants us to leave a great legacy for our children and grandchildren.

Ernest Hemingway said, *"Today is only one day in all the days that will ever be. But what will happen in all the other days that ever come, depends on what you do today!"*[8]

> *"I am convinced that any suffering we endure is less than nothing compared to the magnitude of glory that is about to be unveiled within us. The entire universe is standing on tiptoe, yearning to see the unveiling of God's glorious sons and daughters! For against its will the universe itself has had to endure the empty futility resulting from the consequences of human sin. But now, with eager expectation, all creation longs for freedom from its slavery to decay and to experience with us the wonderful freedom coming to God's children."* Romans 8:18-21 (TPT)

We give God the glory for all that has happened, and we look to Him for completion of what has begun.

---

8. Ernest Hemingway, *For Whom the Bell Tolls* (Charles Scribner's Sons, 1940)

THE PROGRAM CONTINUED

There was a call to repentance by Apostle Tekper on behalf of the Pentecostal Church.

Ali read 2 Chronicles 7:11-15:

> *"When Solomon had finished the temple of the Lord and the royal palace, and had succeeded in carrying out all he had in mind to do in the temple of the Lord and in his own palace, the Lord appeared to him at night and said: "I have heard your prayer and have chosen this place for myself as a temple for sacrifices. When I shut up the heavens so that there is no rain, or command locusts to devour the land or send a plague among my people, if my people, who are called by my name, will humble themselves and pray and seek my face and turn from their wicked ways, then I will hear from heaven, and I will forgive their sin and will heal their land. Now my eyes will be open and my ears attentive to the prayers offered in this place".*

STATEMENT OF APOLOGY FROM THE ECCLESIA LED BY ARCHBISHOP JUSTICE OFEI AKROFI.

This was the climax of this gathering and of all the work to date.

> "The Body of Christ in Cape Coast and the Central Region of Ghana, as well as the whole nation of Ghana, wish to apologise profoundly to all people and families in Ghana. To everyone who was affected or died due to the inhumane treatment of fellow Ghanaian ancestors, who up to 500 years ago sold or perpetuated or collaborated with Western partners to sell their own for whatever reason.
>
> Today we openly apologise for seeing ourselves only as victims, when we sold our own and allowed this to happen. We recognise this is completely unacceptable, we unreservedly repent and we ask for God's forgiveness and your forgiveness.

We acknowledge that people were forcefully removed from their homes and loved ones. They were taken to the slave markets up and down the country where they were sold against their will to be taken overseas. We repent and apologise.

We are ashamed and regret the pain caused, the wrenching apart and disruption of families, husbands from wives and children from parents, affecting all levels of human relationships. For the generations lost, for the tears shed, the misery caused. For the mental, spiritual and physical distress felt; The ill health, broken hearts and premature deaths caused, for broken dreams and the disruption of people's lives.

For the sin and the repercussions of the blood shed of millions of innocent people on our soil, for those killed on our land and in our sea . . . we repent and apologise. We recognise as with Abel's blood, the blood of those ancestors taken has been crying out for 500 years to God . . . This is a grievous sin and we humbly cry out to God in repentance and apologise.

We recognise that the church was complicit – worshipping in the building above the dungeons, whilst our brothers and sisters suffered below. Our women were stripped naked, paraded for selection to be raped by the governor and his men, often impregnated. When the children were born, they were given Western names and carried an air of superiority breeding further division and disunity. We repent and apologise.

For the curses that have been spoken by those taken, causing the Cape Coast Region to repress in its development. For our sin which has suppressed God's plans for Cape Coast as a town. We are truly sorry.

We recognise that as a result of our sin, doors have been opened to the demonic – especially an orphan spirit and poverty spirit. This has given the enemy access to attack us and our descendants causing a lack of progress, ill health, hunger, learning difficulties, poverty, sexual immorality, powerlessness, quarrelling, fighting and a lack of identity and unity. We repent and apologise.

We give thanks that the church brought the Gospel. However, we are so sorry for misusing God's word, in ignorance, to endorse slavery and we repent for using Scripture to manipulate and control.

The church, the Body of Christ in this part of the world makes an unreserved apology to our brothers and sisters affected by the slave trade, some who have returned back home, others still in other lands and those who have died.

The church, the Body of Christ makes an unreserved apology from Cape Coast and the Central Region for its involvement in the slave trade.

We apologise for the continued effects on black communities taken to the shores of the Caribbean, the U.S.A and Europe. The church is hereby committed to working closely with all partners and those countries who have been burdened with carrying the effects of the slave trade.

The World Economic Forum estimated in 2017 that there were 45 million men, women and children trapped in slavery. By the blood of Jesus, we take authority over the sin of our ancestors that may have resulted in the seeds sown for the modern-day slave trade and people trafficking. We ask the Lord to sever and uproot the modern slave trade wherever it is operating.

All this has been made possible today because of the example of Liverpool which was heavily involved in the slave trade. Liverpool did not want to enter this new millennium with a burden of the sin of the slave trade on the city. In 1999, after many years of prayer and cries of repentance the Leader of Liverpool City Council, the Anglican Bishop of Liverpool and others issued a Declaration of Repentance to the whole world.

This apology that we are giving today is a direct response from Liverpool's example and today you see representatives of Liverpool here with us on this journey. So, we would like to extend love, forgiveness, reconciliation, restoration and unity to Liverpool for their bravery in stepping out and their willingness to support others who want to follow their example. God has used this example from Liverpool to open our eyes, so that today, we too in Cape Coast can come to the point when we can apologise to the world for our lack of initiative in standing against the wrong and being accomplices in the slave trade. We recognise and accept Liverpool's apology from 1999 and we not only release forgiveness to you but we also repent and apologise for our part.

We choose to forgive ourselves and those from our land and other lands who have perpetrated this grievous sin. We ask those who have been the victims of this to forgive us and to be reconciled to us. We ask God to forgive us and to bring reconciliation, restoration and healing.

Amen."

There was then a response from the Diaspora Community:

"We recognise and acknowledge the deep apology from the church recognising Africa's rape and enslavement of fellow African's. Every journey of 1,000 years begins with the first step. The church played a significant role in the slave trade which they morally justified, as they worshipped in the church, meeting above the dungeons as those below screamed and cried out. They believed that the African people enslaved were inferior and God had ordained slavery. Our people lost everything, their names, language, families and homes. We hope that the Apology will be backed up with action."

Communion was a powerful time for everyone as we gathered together from across the church and community to eat at the Lord's Table. There was such a strong sense of God's presence.

Sadly, the Afro-American contingent were so full of anger that they chose not to participate in communion or to join us as we moved across to the Cape Coast Slave Castle. Only God's grace can enable people to forgive such atrocities committed against their ancestors. We need to continue to pray for all those so deeply affected, that one day there will be reconciliation and healing for them.

The procession to the "Door of No Return" in Cape Coast Slave Castle (just across the road), was incredible! Kofi encouraged everyone to walk across in pairs holding hands, singing "Amazing Grace". As we filed through the entrance gates and down towards the "Door of No Return" we had no idea of the massive moment in history that was unfolding before our very eyes and that God Himself had enabled us to be a tiny part of it. We were there for such a time as this! Wow!

We walked across the stone pavement with a freedom to choose to come back, unlike all those precious Africans who entered with no free will.We walked together so aware of the violence and bloodshed. What horrific stories could be told if these very stones could tell their tales!

The priests and church leaders stood in the tunnel leading to the "Door of No Return", as though it was a "fire tunnel" but instead this time it was a tunnel of repentance. People filed through the tunnel and the "Door of No Return" until they were standing looking out at the turbulent ocean. All around us there where the fishermen cleaning and mending their nets almost oblivious of the incredible event unfolding before them.

We held a minute's silence to remember all those who had died before further prayers of intercession and repentance were led by the Roman Catholic priest. Apostle Osae then stepped forward to lead prayers of confession and repentance.

Pastor Spaine then poured the remnants of the communion wine into the sea and on to the land as a prophetic act for cleansing. He took a few moments to explain what he was doing and why he was doing it. This wine represented the covering of the blood of Jesus:

> *"You have come to God, the Judge of all, to the spirits of the righteous made perfect, to Jesus the mediator of a new covenant, and to the sprinkled blood that speaks a better word than the blood of Abel".*
> Hebrews 12:23

All of a sudden, the weather seemed to respond to what was happening and the clouds swirled releasing their rain gently over us all for a few moments.

The closing statement was given by Cape Coast Metropolitan Assembly (CCMA)/Regional Administration, the Mayor. We had been expecting a general statement but when Ernest Arthur the mayor and chief executive of the CCMA stepped up, we were all taken by surprise. He also began to read an incredible Statement of Repentance on behalf of the authority of Cape Coast.

Kofi then led us all in making a declaration based on Isaiah 61:

> In the name of Jesus I declare and decree: "The Spirit of the Sovereign Lord is on me, because the Lord has anointed and commissioned me to proclaim good news to the poor. He has sent me to bind up the broken-hearted, to proclaim freedom for the captives and release from darkness for the prisoners".

We will step out of the shadows and encourage everyone we know to step out of the shadows of the slave trade. We declare the orphan spirit and the spirit of poverty is broken off our nation. It is time for Ghana to step into freedom.

We declare this is the year of the Lord's favour for our lives, for our families and for our nation. It is time for us to receive and wear a crown of beauty instead of ashes, the oil of joy instead of mourning, and a garment of praise instead of a spirit of despair. Ghana will be called righteous, strong, magnificent, distinguished for integrity, justice and a planting of the Lord for the display of his splendour.

We declare we will rebuild the ancient ruins and restore the places long devastated. We will no longer be ashamed, we will receive a double portion, and instead of disgrace we will rejoice in our inheritance. We will inherit a double portion in our land, and everlasting joy will be ours. Amen.

VERONICA THEN DECLARED "A NEW EDICT – I HAVE A DREAM."

We had written a new edict reversing and cancelling the previous edicts over Cape Coast and the Central Region. (You can use this for your community too.)

I have a dream for my beloved city of Cape Coast and the Central
Region where:
People understand who God created them to be
and live in their destiny.
Where people care for one another
and people are welcomed and loved.
Where Biblical marriage is honoured and precious.
Where children can grow up in a safe home
with a Mother and Father who love and care for them.
Where there is no poverty –
physically, financially and spiritually.

Where there is no orphan spirit.
Where our elderly people are cherished and honoured.

Where there is no gang violence.
No racism or hatred because people are different.
Where there are no murders or violent acts
or bullying, manipulation or control.

Where there is no domestic violence,
no street prostitution, brothels or sexual exploitation.
Where there are no addictions . . .
alcohol, drugs, pornography, gambling etc.
Where we have a police force without corruption.
Where the local government govern with heavens strategies.
Where our environment is clean and healthy.

Where nobody goes hungry
or is left outside on the streets, homeless
and where all people have suitable homes.
Where all people have sound and healthy minds
and there are no suicides or self-harming.

Where the media is edifying, unbiased and truthful.
Where justice is honest and fair.
Where education enables and empowers
everyone to reach their potential.

Where Jesus truly is Lord
and every other faith group has bowed the knee to Jesus.
Where there are no idols.
Where the church is full of people
who love God and love to worship Him.
Where there is a sense of belonging
and nobody is left isolated.

Where the church is led
by anointed leadership teams operating in their gifts.
Where leaders are appointed by God and not man.
Where the church lives to glorify the King.

I have a God who loves my city of Cape Coast
and the Central Region
and the people who live, work and visit.
I have a God who will be glorified in Cape Coast
and the Central Region
and who can make the impossible possible . . .

Veronica continued: "Ephesians 3:16-20, Passion Translation says:

"I pray that Father God would unveil within you the unlimited riches of his glory and favour until supernatural strength floods your innermost being with his divine might and explosive power. Then, by constantly using your faith, the life of Christ will be released deep inside you, and the resting place of his love will become the very source and root of your life.

Then you will be empowered to discover what every holy one experiences – the great magnitude of the astonishing love of Christ in all its dimensions. How deeply intimate and far-reaching is His love! How enduring and inclusive it is! Endless love beyond measurement that transcends our understanding, this extravagant love pours into you until you are filled to overflowing with the fullness of God!

Never doubt God's mighty power to work in you and accomplish all this. He will achieve infinitely more than your greatest request, your most unbelievable dream, and exceed your wildest imagination! He will outdo them all, for his miraculous power constantly energizes you."

So, I have a dream. What is your dream for Cape Coast and the Central Region? We can have a dream that can one day become a reality. Let us promise God, promise ourselves and promise Cape Coast and the Central Region that we will pray for the prosperity of this land. If Cape Coast and the Central Region prospers, we too will prosper. So be it God!

Kofi Annan said, "To live is to choose. But to choose well, you must know who you are and what you stand for, where you want to go and why you want to get there". Let us choose life today!"

Archbishop Justice led the closing prayer and final blessing.

Time for business

Wow! Wow! What an incredibly powerful time. This was the beginning of a mighty shift and we were all really encouraged.

Our team were invited for lunch with Ernest Arthur, the Mayor and Chief Executive of the Cape Coast Metropolitan Assembly back at our hotel. We were joined by John Manwell, Christopher Gibaud, Marcus Jeremy and Papa Fasanya who shared their hearts to connect with the business leaders and to help in the days ahead.

Sunday morning was the start of the Jewish new year and it was as though the birds had understood and chose to sing a new "Hallelujah" chorus to awaken us. We had an early breakfast before making our way to the cathedral for our final service. Bishop Victor invited us to join them all for lunch afterwards, but we decided it would be best just to pop in to say "Goodbye" and get back on the road to Accra. The journey this time was fairly uneventful, except for seeing a tall guy climbing into a skip completely naked! You do see some sights when travelling in Africa!

PRAYER: Heavenly Father I want to make myself available to be used by you. Help me to see my community the way that you see it. Help me to pray for my community the way that Jesus is praying for it. Help me to be a vessel to bring heaven to earth. Amen.

Divine Appointments

We realised when we got home, that the video footage we had taken of The Apology at Cape Coast, was really important. I could put something together on my laptop, but I was concerned it would not be good enough quality. Ali and I prayed and asked God to help us to produce the best video we could with what we had filmed. On our first Sunday home, Ali was coming out of church when she met an American lady who had just started attending the church whilst Ali was in Ghana. Ali introduced herself and soon discovered that Revis Meeks had just moved to St Helens from Hollywood. Revis was a Hollywood TV sub-editor and had helped to produce many TV series. Before they separated Ali had told her all about our little movie and Revis had very kindly offered her services to help us.

A few days later we were working together huddled around my laptop looking at the footage and making decisions about what should be in the movie and what should not be. We added some music in a couple of places and then finally, when we had done as much as we could with Revis, we all realised that we really could do with the help of a sound engineer. The video had been recorded with a mixture of Ali's iPhone and my camera but with no special microphones to help us pick up the sound clearly. We suddenly realised that we had access to one of the best BBC sound engineers in the country. We called our friend Steve Brooke, who is part of the CWM Team and works for the BBC. Steve had recently been recognised by the BBC for the "Best use of sound". So, God answered our prayer with a Hollywood film editor and an award-winning BBC sound engineer!!! He is certainly the God of breakthrough in so many ways.

You can watch the film for yourself on: https://youtu.be/v_xa_KfJspQ

Sometimes when you are in the middle of situations, you recognise they are very important, but it is often only when you pause to reflect that you realise the breakthrough is actually much bigger than you grasped. As we reflected on The Apology in the weeks after, we realised that we needed to tell this story back in Liverpool. In five hundred years since the transatlantic slave trade, no other city had ever repented and been forgiven before and we needed to tell this incredible side of the story.

Liverpool is the home of The International Slavery Museum, opened on 23rd August 2007. Not only was this the date of the annual Slavery Remembrance Day, but the year 2007 was particularly significant as it was the bicentenary of the abolition of the British slave trade. The museum highlights the international horror of slavery, both in a historic and contemporary context. Working in partnership with other museums to provides opportunities for greater awareness and understanding of the legacy of slavery today.

It is located in Liverpool's Albert Dock, at the centre of a World Heritage site and only yards away from the dry docks where 18th century slave trading ships were repaired and fitted out.

We made an appointment to meet Dr Richard Benjamin who leads the work at the International Slavery Museum. Archbishop Justice, Maria and I had a wonderful meeting with Dr Benjamin telling him the story and leaving him with a copy of The Apology. We talked about the possibility of how this story could be told within the museum at some point in the future. We were given a personal tour and came away very encouraged.

A few weeks later we had an appointment with the Mayor of Liverpool, Joe Anderson. Archbishop Justice, Maria, Ali and I were warmly greeted by Joe and his team. They had a media team there filming and taking photos as we told the story and presented Joe with a copy of The Apology. It is important to understand that as Liverpool was forgiven, it began to lift off the power of any curses that were made over the land, and to release further blessings.

We had a good conversation with Joe, and he talked about the possibility of Liverpool twinning with Cape Coast and what that may look like. He could see conversations developing between the two police forces, the museums working together, education and the churches. To date those things have not happened yet but these things take time and we only want God's timing.

PRAYER: God I give you all the glory for every breakthrough in my life. I pray that you will help me to be a vessel that you can use to bring breakthrough in my life, my family, in my ministry, in my community and in my nation. Amen.

From Isolation To Mobilisation

As I am writing this, extravagant breakthroughs are happening on a mammoth scale! I want to share some prophetic revelation and to describe the situation we are actually in.

In January 2020 God said to me, "This will be a season of choosing between religious life with its frustrations or Kingdom life where we allow the King to determine our vision and direction. This season and decade will see the doors of many churches closing, and many will not reopen because they no longer have life. When that happens God will release leaders into their next season of life and make way for buildings to be reopened with a fresh move of God's Spirit".

On 5th March 2020, the first death due to coronavirus was reported in the UK. Whilst there was great concern about this, clearly nobody comprehended what was starting to unfold.

On 15th March 2020, during a time of worship in church, I had a very vivid vision and I could see many people, in fact multitudes, coming one by one into the valley of decision. Then I began to sing prophetically, "Every knee will bow, and every tongue will confess that Jesus Christ is Lord". I knew we were poised on the verge of something very powerful and I went to the front of church to share what I had seen.

However, as soon as I had finished sharing, the presence of God came upon me so heavily as I staggered back to my seat. I could not stand or even sit down, so I settled down onto the floor. Next the Lord came upon me even more powerfully and He showed me two visions.

In the first vision, God was violently taking hold of clay and slamming it hard on to the potter's wheel. He said that He is reforming us as individuals and reforming the church. He is not putting a new handle on it or repainting it. He is slamming it on to the potter's wheel and handling it to remove the bubbles and the impurities. We say, *"Yes Lord"*, but next comes the firing of the pot! If there are impurities in the pot as it goes into the fire, it will crack and break.

> *"This is the word that came to Jeremiah from the Lord: "Go down to the potter's house, and there I will give you my message." So I went down to the potter's house, and I saw him working at the wheel. But the pot he was shaping from the clay was marred in his hands; so the potter formed it into another pot, shaping it as seemed best to him."*
> Jeremiah 18:1-4

Are we truly willing and prepared for what God is doing to make us fit to be the Bride for His Beloved Son? When we are prepared to yield to God in this season we will come out of this looking like the Bride, smelling like the Bride, living like the Bride and loving like the Bride.

> *"Come," say the Holy Spirit and the Bride in divine duet. Let everyone who hears this duet join them in saying, "Come". Let everyone gripped with spiritual thirst say, "Come". And let everyone who craves the gift of living water come and drink it freely. "It is my gift to you! Come."*
> Revelation 22:17 (TPT)

A few moments later, I saw a vision of a carpet heaped over so much rubbish that had been getting swept under it for years. Individuals and churches had been just lifting the edge and sweeping their sin under, out of sight and out of mind, to enable them to carry on as normal, some for many years. I saw Satan standing victorious on the top of it all. He was victorious because individuals and the corporate church had unknowingly handed their authority over to him, because they chose unrighteousness over dealing with their sin. For that is what it is when we sweep sin under the carpet and turn a blind eye, until we become blind to the truth. I saw the Lord giving us all a window of time and a window of love, grace and mercy to lift the rug and deal with the rubbish. In the vision as people began to repent, forgive and deal with their sin, I saw Satan simply standing on the carpet. Then I saw the Lord come and He said that He was going to pull the rug from under Satan's feet! He bent down and violently pulled the rug from under Satan's feet and once again restored the authority to His people and to His Bride!

Since then we have seen everything that can be shaken shaking. Prime Minister Boris Johnson announced a LOCK DOWN across the UK on 24th March 2020. This has meant that most people have not been able to go out of their homes except for essential shopping or essential services working. The decision to do that was based on trying to preserve our National Health Service so they are not overwhelmed by the number of people seriously ill with the coronavirus. There is no doubt that suddenly we have all found ourselves in the middle of an unprecedented, global and catastrophic pandemic – an emergency which is impacting everyone!

Suddenly everyone was impacted, from the poorest of the poor to members of the Royal family, even our own Prime Minister Boris Johnson was very poorly in Intensive Care for several days. People from every walk of life and almost every nation have been infected. To date, millions have been infected and around three-quarters of a million deaths have been reported globally! Clearly those figures are not going to be completely accurate and sadly will continue to rise in the days ahead.

People have died isolated from their families and loved ones because of the severity of the infection. Hospitals and national governments have been in crisis, scrambling for solutions as they have watched businesses collapsing, money markets crashing, weddings being postponed, funerals limited to immediate family only, people fighting over toilet rolls and non-essential workers being isolated in their homes.

The church buildings and many of the things that have occupied our time have been closed. Now is the time to make the main things the main things! It is scary because we are not in control and much is being stripped away, until our focus is on Jesus. It is time for us to repent of our sin, forgive where we need to, be re-formed, re-fuelled and re-fired for the coming season.

Turning point – 8 minutes and 46 seconds

There are moments in history that are real turning points when there is momentum for things that have never shifted before to suddenly shift quickly and powerfully. Tragically despite the murder of many black people in America and other nations, little has been done about it, because of so much racism. However, this time was different when on 25th May 2020, a 46-year-old man called George Floyd was murdered in Minneapolis. What was different was that as police officers murdered George Floyd while he was handcuffed on the floor, this was filmed. Two officers held him down, the third knelt on his neck for 8 minutes and 45 seconds, whilst George called out for his mother and cried, "I can't breathe!" The fourth police officer stood by to ensure nobody attempted to intervene.

Shockwaves have gone right around the world, with protests in many nations. The carpet has been lifted on racism and it has been swept out for all to see. The history and influence of the transatlantic slave trade upon Afro-Americans and others has come to the surface on a massive scale for all to see.

Conversations and prayer meetings have been happening all across the nations, as the world grapples with the horror of what has been happening for far too long. Liverpool, as a historical slave port, has been responding too with peaceful protest marches and challenges to areas of our history that have not yet been dealt with. Watch this space, as God is moving very powerfully.

May God have mercy on us and may we all ensure our hearts are cleansed ready for the fire! The church will emerge re-prioritised and what will emerge will be beautiful, powerfully anointed and will understand the significance of intimacy with God. Many people will encounter God afresh and many for the first time. People will be compelled by God's love to share the good news, of hope, peace and joy to those entering the valley of decision.

We will encounter Emmanuel, God with us, in the tough days and the great days. We will experience a new season as the Church takes off the army boots and, in the place of intimacy with the King of Kings, the Bride will put on her Gospel shoes of peace. Soon a truly infectious revival will happen as the Spirit and the Bride say COME!!!

The book is called *Extravagant Breakthroughs* because it tells the stories of very ordinary people who have done what they can do, accompanied by an incredible extravagant God who brings the breakthroughs. I encourage you to do all God calls you to do and then watch what He does!

Today's breakthroughs are tomorrow's legacies!

And finally, Numbers 6:24 has become an anthem that has been shared all around the world:

> *"The Lord bless you and keep you; the Lord make his face shine on you and be gracious to you; the Lord turn his face toward you and give you peace".* Amen.

PRAYER: Heavenly Father I place my life on the potter's wheel, and I ask that you re-model me. I lift the carpet and choose to sweep out everything that has been hidden that has given Satan authority in my life and ministry. I ask that you help me to be part of Jesus' Bride, to live like the Bride, to look like the Bride, smell like the Bride, and to love like the Bride. I pray that I will choose to wear the Gospel shoes of peace and bring the Gospel that cost your precious son Jesus His life, to as many people as I can. Amen.

You can connect with what we are doing via www.cwmprayer.com or our Facebook page CWM